Light Me Down

ALSO BY JEAN VALENTINE

Poetry

Shirt in Heaven
Break the Glass
Little Boat
Door in the Mountain: New and Collected Poems, 1965–2003
The Cradle of the Real Life
Growing Darkness, Growing Light
The Under Voice: Selected Poems
The River at Wolf
Home Deep Blue: New and Selected Poems
The Messenger
Ordinary Things
Pilgrims
Dream Barker

Translations

Dark Elderberry Branch: Poems of Marina Tsvetaeva

Chapbooks

Friend
[the Ship]
Lucy

Anthologies Edited

The Lighthouse Keeper: Essays on the Poetry of Eleanor Ross Taylor

Light Me Down

The New & Collected Poems of

Jean Valentine

FOREWORD BY ANNE MARIE MACARI

Alice James Books
NEW GLOUCESTER, MAINE
alicejamesbooks.org

© 2024 by the Jean Valentine Literary Estate
All rights reserved
Printed in the United States

10 9 8 7 6 5 4 3 2 1

Alice James Books are published by Alice James Poetry Cooperative, Inc.

Alice James Books
Auburn Hall
60 Pineland Drive, Suite 206
New Gloucester, ME 04260
www.alicejamesbooks.org

Library of Congress Cataloging-in-Publication Data

Names: Valentine, Jean, author. | Macari, Anne Marie, writer of foreword.
Title: Light me down : the new & collected poems of Jean Valentine / foreword by Anne Marie Macari.
Other titles: Light me down (Compilation)
Description: New Gloucester, Maine : Alice James Books, 2024. | Includes index.
Identifiers: LCCN 2023039806 (print) | LCCN 2023039807 (ebook) | ISBN 9781949944600 (hardcover) | ISBN 9781949944594 (paperback) | ISBN 9781949944327 (e-book)
Subjects: LCGFT: Poetry.
Classification: LCC PS3572.A39 L54 2024 (print) | LCC PS3572.A39 (ebook) | DDC 811/.54223/eng/20231002--dcundefined
LC record available at https://lccn.loc.gov/2023039806
LC ebook record available at https://lccn.loc.gov/2023039807

Alice James Books gratefully acknowledges support from individual donors, private foundations, and the National Endowment for the Arts.

Front cover photo: Portrait of Jean Valentine, 1967-1968. Radcliffe College Archives. Schlesinger Library, Harvard Radcliffe Institute. Front cover texture: Shutterstock / Akura Yochi.

Back/spine cover photo by Joanne Eldridge Morrissey

CONTENTS

Foreword

New Poems (2016–2020)

Light Me Down	1
The Ring	2
To My Teacher	3
Thirst	4
Image:	5
Trust me	6
Pneumonia, January	7
Dear Adrienne	8
Yeats' Stance	9
The Teacher	10
The Cricket	11
Sparrow	12
Trust	13
In a Diner	14
For Tomas Tranströmer &	
Max Ritvo	15
February, 2017	16
The Longing	17
The 40's	18
Poem with a Line from	
Ko Un	19
Dear Merton's God	20
In Ireland	21
In China	22
For a friend who died young	23
"Regard all dharmas as	
dreams"	24
For Monty	25
A minute of silence for	
C.D. Wright	26

The Prison	27
After Fernando Traverso	28
Here	29

Dream Barker (1965)

First Love	33
For a Woman Dead at Thirty	33
Miles from Home	34
To Salter's Point	35
Lines in Dejection	36
Sleep Drops Its Nets	37
Déjà-vu	37
Sunset at Wellfleet	38
Asleep over Lines from	
Willa Cather	38
Cambridge by Night	39
To a Friend	40
Waiting	41
Sasha and the Poet	43
The Second Dream	43
A Bride's Hours	43
1. Dawn	43
2. The Bath	44
3. Night	44
Afterbirth	45
Sarah's Christening Day	46
Tired of London	46
Cambridge, April 27, 1957	47
New York, April 27, 1962	48
September 1963	49
Riverside	49
For Teed	50

My Grandmother's Watch	51	Coltrane, Syeeda's Song Flute	90
The Beast with Two Backs	52	Photograph of Delmore	
The Little Flower	54	Schwartz	91
Sex	63	The Torn-down Building	92
Adam and Eve: Poem on		Moon Man	93
Folded Paper	63	The Child and the Terrorist,	
Dream Barker	64	The Terrorist and	
To My Soul	65	the Child	94
		Night	95
		Pilgrims	96

Pilgrims (1969)

I

The Couples	71	
Fireside	71	
Solomon	72	
In the Museum	73	
By the Boat Pond	74	
The Summer House	75	
Woods	76	
Her dream: the child	77	
Orpheus and Eurydice	77	
Goodbye	79	
Separation	79	
Thinking about Cain	82	
Dearest,	82	

II

April	83
Broken-down Girl	84
Bin Dream, West College	
East, D-II	85
Bin Dream #2, Interview	
with Stravinsky	85
Death House	86
Archangel	87
Half an Hour	87
Visiting Day at School	89
The Child Jung	90

Ordinary Things (1974)

I

After Elegies	101
'Autumn Day'	101
He said,	102
Forces	103
Kin	103
Anesthesia	104
After Elegies (2)	104

II

3 A.M. in New York	105
Space	105
Letter from a Country Room	106
A Child's Death	107
Revolution	108
Three Voices One Night in the	
Community Kitchen	108
The Knife	109
Seeing *L'Atalante*	110

III

"Twenty Days' Journey" by	
Huub Oosterhuis translated	
from the Dutch with	
Judith Herzberg	111

IV

This Hate	115
This Minute	116
Couvre-Feu: after Paul Eluard	118
Fidelities	119
Susan's Photograph	121
Outside the Frame	122
Forces (2): Song	122

The Messenger (1979)

The Messenger

Beka, 14	125
Dufy Postcard	125
The Field	126
Living Together	127
Here Now	128
The Forgiveness Dream: Man from the Warsaw Ghetto	129
Turn	130
Prayer in Fever	131
Working	132
Silences: A Dream of Governments	133
After Elegies (3)	134
The Messenger	135

Two Translations

Huub Oosterhuis: Orpheus	139
Osip Mandelstam: 394	141

Solitudes

December 21st	143
Sanctuary	144
What Happened	145
Turn (2): After Years	147
The Burden of Memory	148

February 9th	150
"Love and Work": Freud Dying	153
Letter from a Stranger	154
"Actuarial File"	154
Lines from a Story	156
March 21st	157

Home.Deep.Blue (1989)

Willi, Home	163
To Raphael, angel of happy meeting	163
Primitive Painting: Liberation Day	164
Awake, This Summer	165
Mandelstam	166
The Drinker's Wife Writes Back	167
Birthday Letter from South Carolina	167
The Counselor Retires, and Then He Dies	168
Juliana	169
Visit	170
Snow Landscape, in a Glass Globe	171
Everything Starts with a Letter	172
About Love	173
Little Song in Indian Summer	174
The King	174
High School Boyfriend	175
Tonight I Can Write.	175
Trust Me	176

The River At Wolf (1992)

X	181
Spring and Its Flowers	181
The Summer Was Not	
Long Enough	182
Still Life, for Matisse	183
Still Life: in the Epidemic	183
Ikon	185
The Year of the Snake	185
The One You Wanted to Be	
Is the One You Are	186
Ironwood	187
Bud	187
To a Young Poet	188
Foraging	188
Alfred and the Abortion	189
Redemption	190
Seeing You	191
The Free Abandonment	
Blues	192
The First Station	193
Night Lake	194
The Badlands Said	195
The Missouri Speaks	195
The River at Wolf	196
The Ring	197
Barrie's Dream, the	
Wild Geese	197
Fox Glacier	198
Lindis Pass, Borage	198
By the Tekapo River,	
100 Degrees	199
After Consciousness of	
This Big Form	199
Everyone Was Drunk	200
In Fear (1)	201
In Fear (2)	201
In This Egg	201
The Under Voice	202

Come Ahkmatova	203
James Wright: in Memory	203
Wish-Mother	204
At Cullens' Island	204
The Wisdom Gravy	205
American River Sky	
Alcohol Father	205
The Morning of	
My Mother's Death	206
The Night of	
My Mother's Death	206
Second Mother	207
The Sea of Serenity	208
My Mother's Body, My Professor,	
My Bower	208
Butane	209
At My Mother's Grave	209
We Go Through Our	
Mother's Things	210
Death Ashphodel	210
To the Memory of	
David Kalstone	211
The First Angel	211
At the Door	212
Yield Everything,	
Force Nothing	212
Alone, Alive	213
Flower	214
Skate	214
Guardian Angel in New York	215
To Plath, to Sexton	215
The Power Table	216

Growing Darkness, Growing Light
**   (1997)**

Rain	221
Sick, Away from Home	221
Friend	222

Homesick	222
New Life	223
Bees	223
The Tractors	223
River Jordan	224
Night Porch	224
*	
World-light	225
Snow Family	226
To the Black Madonna	
of Chartres	226
Tell Me, What Is the Soul	227
Mastectomy	227
Secret Room, Danger House	228
Red for Blood	228
Yellow for Gold	229
Green for the Land	229
Black for the People	230
Home	231
Long Irish Summer Day	231
*	
Dog Skin Coat	232
Fellini in Purgatory	233
Elegy for Jane Kenyon	233
You Are Not One in	
a Sequence	234
Alcohol	234
Where Do You Look for Me?	235
Documentary: AIDS	
Support Group	235
Poem with Words by	
Thornton Dial	235
A Bit of Rice	236
The Night of Wally's Service,	
Wally Said,	236
Rodney Dying	237
Rodney Dying (2)	237
Father Lynch Returns from	
the Dead	238
The Baby Rabbits in	

the Garden	238
*	
Mother and Child, Body	
and Soul	239
Soul	240
Soul (2)	240
The Mother Dreams	241
Fistula	242
Soul (3)	242
*	
Open Heart	243
Listening	245

The Cradle of the Real Life (2000)

Part 1

The Pen	251
Elegy for Jane Kenyon (2)	251
Black Wolf	252
Mother Bones	253
They lead me	253
Your mouth "appeared	
to me"	254
Mare and Newborn Foal	254
Truth	255
October Premonition	255
Rodney Dying (3)	256
November	256
Labrador	256
1945	257
Leaving	258
Running for a train	258
The Welsh poet	259
Radio: Poetry Reading, NPR	259
The Tower Roof	260
For a Women Dead	
at Thirty (2)	260
The Blind Stirring of Love	261
Little Map	262

The Drinker	262	The Coin	293
The Drinker (2)	263	October morning	294
Happiness	264	I heard my left hand	294
Happiness (2): The I Ching	264	In the evening	294
He leaves them:	265	*	
Away from you	265	We cut the new day	295
Child	266	Occurrence of White	296
		How have I hurt you?	296
Part II: Her Lost Book		Do flies remember us	297
1.	266	You drew my head	297
2.	271	The little, faintly blue	
3.	276	clay eggs	298
		Happiness (3)	298
		Letter	299
Door in the Mountain (2004)		I could never let go	299
		The Basket House	300
Annunciation	283	The House and the World	301
*		In your eyes	302
In our child house	283	Woman, Leaving	302
Nine	283	Trim my hoofs	302
The girl	284	Two Poems for	
Mother	285	Matthew Shepard	303
Eighteen	285	The Blue Dory, the Soul	304
"She Sang"	286	The Rally	304
A Bone Standing Up	287	The Growing Christ	
The Hawthorn Robin Mends		of Tzintzuntzan	305
with Thorns	287	Sheep	305
Out in a sailboat	287	To the Bardo	306
I came to you	288	Rodney Dying (4)	306
*		*	
Cousin	289	Door in the Mountain	307
The Very Bad Horse	289	Monarch butterfly	307
Once	290	My old body	308
So many secrets	290	Inkwell daybreak	308
Eleventh Brother	291	The path between	308
Once in the nights	291	The Night Sea	309
Under the gold	291	The Shirt	309
The Windows	292	One Foot in the Dark	310
Go Clear	293	A weed green	310

Fears: Night Cabin	310	Once I was girls and boys	330
so wild	311	The Eleventh Brother (2)	330
I have lived in your face	311	"Remote Objects of	
A goldfinch in the rain	312	Intense Devotion"	331
The grain of the wood	312	The first thing	332
The push or fly	312	That I had treated you badly	332
I would be	313	Day & Night	333
Avalon	313	All around the outside	333
Do you remember?	314		
Advent Calendar	314	**Jesus Said,**	
We didn't know each other	315	The Woman's Poem	334
Touch with your finger	315	Annunciation Poem	335
Noon in the Line Outside	315	The Poet's Poem	335
Inside	316	The Teacher's Poem	336
Your number is lifting off		Death Poem	336
my hand	316	The Afterlife Poem	336
*			
The Needle North	317	**Strange Lights**	
The Passing	317	Hospital: far from home	337
In the Burning Air	318	Hospital: *At last*	337
Little house	318	Hospital: strange lights	338
		Hospital: It was euphoria	339
		Hospital: Scraps	339
Little Boat (2007)		**A Bowl Of Milk**	
		The Look	340
La Chalupa, the Boat	323	I wanted to be sure to	
		reach you	340
For her	323	When she told me	341
The Artist in Prison	324	This Side	341
In Memory	324	His White Jade Eggs	342
But your touch	325	I was lying there	342
The Poet	326	The Harrowing	343
Photographs at her Wake	326		
Mattress on the floor:	327	**From the Questions of Bhanu Kapil**	
Lord of the world!	327	Where did you come from/	
The door is fallen down	328	how did you arrive?	344
Door	328	What is the shape of	
The father was a carrier	329	your body?	344
Gray	329		

What do you remember about the earth?	345
What are the consequences of silence?	345
How will you/have you prepare(d) for your death?	346

Maria Gravida, Mary Expectant

Maria Gravida	346
Eye of water	347
Moose and calf	347
To my soul (2)	348
The Rose	348

Break the Glass (2010)

I

In prison	351
The whitewashed walls	352
The Leopard	352
Even all night long	353
I was working	354
"As with rosy steps the morn"	354
Dear Family,	355
Canoe	356
The Japanese garden	356
Ghost Elephants	357
On a Passenger Ferry	358
Then Abraham	358
Traveler	359
Coyote	359
Hawkins Stable	360

II

Who watches	360
Time is matter here	361
Earth and the Librarian	361
Her car	362

The World inside This One	362
Poet	363
(Two were seen leaving.)	363
The treeless hill	364
The just-born rabbits	364
The valley	365
On the bus	365
The branches	366
Red cloth	366

III

Don't silence yourself, _No te calles_	367
Eurydice who guides	367
If a Person Visits Someone in a Dream, in Some Cultures the Dreamer Thanks Them	368
I dropped a plate	369
Desert Prison	370
You ask,	371
The Young Mother	371
I thought It's time	372
On the CD, in the rainstorm	372
Old love, I want to phone you	373
Diana	373
The older man among us	374
He Disappeared into Complete Silence	374
I am fain a page in the court of space	375

IV

Lucy	375

Shirt in Heaven (2015)

Luna Moth

Luna Moth	387

A Child's Drawing, 1941	387
1943: The Vision	388
Forest, Stars	388
Her last year	389
God of rooms	389
Hold the finch	390
1945	391
For love,	392
Shirt in Heaven	392
there's nothing when	393
Peace to bad waters	393
Bardo	394
W. 13th Street	395
Open	395
A leaf, a shadow-hand	396
You rope that pulls them where they do not go	396
The helicopter,	397
When I lost my courage	398
His hand takes	398
Bury your money	399
Poem with endwords by Reginald Shepherd	399
She will be	400

Friend

[The ship] is slowly giving up her sentient life, I cannot write about it.	400
Hospice	401
Isn't there something	402
Down on the street	403
Both you & he	403
My words to you	404
I'm going to sleep	404
I'd get you a glass of champagne	405
We turn in dream	405
Are all the things	406
You're gone	406

Then	406
You Speak	407

Threshold

Could it be heat?	408
The Window:	408
The Door:	410
Bellini, Saint Francis	411
In the Famine Museum	411
Friend,	412
Great-grandmother,	413

Then had we well put to, without form, without text

Note in winter	413
Ten Degrees	414
When I woke up, our time	414
When I woke up, my friend	415
Self-Portrait, Rembrandt, 1658	416
Song	416
Icebergs, Ilulissat	417

Notes	419
Acknowledgments	423
Index of Titles	431
Index of First Lines	441

About the Author

FOREWORD

Jean Valentine was a once-in-a-generation poet of the interior life—the Emily Dickinson of our age, by which I mean an essential, deep-lyric poet, an American original, whose unique voice, diction, fragmentation, whose honest dwelling in otherness, cannot be imitated.

Born in 1934, Valentine died from complications of Alzheimer's disease in December 2020, in the middle of the COVID-19 pandemic. She left a stunning body of work now collected in this volume, including new poems she wrote in her last years. Her first book, *Dream Barker and Other Poems*, won the 1964 Yale Younger Poets Prize, and she went on to win, over the course of her lifetime, most of the prestigious awards that a poet can win, including the National Book Award for *Door in the Mountain*, the Shelley Memorial Award from the Poetry Society of America, the Wallace Stevens Award from the Academy of American Poets, and the Bollingen Prize for Poetry from Yale University. She also received numerous fellowships, including from the Guggenheim Foundation, The Rockefeller Foundation, the NEA, and The American Academy of Arts and Letters, among others, and she was the State Poet of New York from 2008-2010.

A Jean Valentine poem transports us, and yet we arrive where she takes us without ever knowing how we got there, only that we have found ourselves beyond the borders of our known world. Only that we have crossed and awakened in some place we knew was there but could never articulate or find by ourselves. Maybe that is the definition of poetry: a mysterious arrival in a place both surprising and yet somehow familiar—and maybe Jean Valentine herself was a living embodiment of poetry—traveling worlds as if nothing separates us, not life or death, not space or time. As if the borders never existed—

> In the electricity of love, its lightning strike
> or in its quiet hum in the thighs
> like this little icebox here
> not knowing any better
> or in the dumb hum of the heater going on
> little stirs in the room-tone
> I rush outdoors into the air you are
> Lucy
> and you rush out to receive me
> At last there you are
> who I always *knew* was there
> but almost died not
> meeting

> From "*Lucy*"

"Lucy" refers to a famous fossil skeleton discovered in Ethiopia in 1974, and in this long, late-career poem, Valentine writes of Lucy as an ancestor, as *the* ancestor. Valentine is forthright about her own mysticism, that connection that she understands is between all things, the energy we are all made of. Writing from that connection, writing from loss, from longing, from the endless searching that births art of all kinds, Valentine pulls us into what so deeply and vulnerably makes us human, claiming *Lucy* as a visceral female deity, one she has long been searching for "but almost died not meeting." In "Lucy" the concerns and questions of her lifetime in poetry come together.

As a teacher, Valentine's advice was straightforward and seemingly simple, but of course enacting that simplicity is not the same as talking about it. She would say—and this is central to her work—"*you don't have to explain in a poem.*" For her it was natural to just be, for the poem to exist as if born whole from her hand and mouth, from her being. She didn't set things up for the reader or prepare the reader, she just transported us to wherever she was going.

Although she said many times that she wrote from her dreams, we never feel we are watching or hearing about someone else's dream. Instead we *awaken* into her dream world, one we recognize, though it is wholly new to us.

She always said that she wanted her poems to be clear, but also mysterious. And as unexpected as her poems can seem, there's a clarity that's not definitive, not boxed in by reason, but approachable, especially if you are willing to learn her language. In that way too she is akin to Dickinson—each poet speaking a personal language, a *slanted* language as Dickinson would say, and we only need to bring wonder and attention to the work in order for the door to slip open and for us to find ourselves inside the poems. Once there, the poems keep opening. Reading after reading, year after year, Valentine's poems grow in us, enliven and alert us, bring our sorrow to the surface and our joy, our desire to truly be in this life but simultaneously in touch with something other, something beyond. Such is great poetry.

Shortly after *Break the Glass* came out in 2010, Valentine was a poet-in-residence at the MFA program at Drew University. Former students from that time still speak of an event where they were asked to prepare questions about her new book. The students were in awe of Jean, as well as in love with her, and they wanted to ask smart questions. One of them started by asking about her use of punctuation. Jean answered quietly but firmly, *"I don't know."* Then another student asked her a question, and she answered with another *"I don't know."* And for the most part, that's how the interview went. Question after question.

Though very uncomfortable in the moment, it was one of the best lessons she could have given us, inviting us into the world of the unknown that is poetry, into the mystery, showing us that our questions won't save us from uncertainty when we face the blank page. Rules or methods won't get us where we need to go. She prepared us to go wherever the poem might lead without having to support it with explanation or theory—she was not interested in theory. She was interested in what was alive in the poem, in the experience, not the idea of the poem. Jean Valentine taught us about silence, patience, wildness, presence—she taught us that *the other* is us.

A note on the New Poems:

I met Jean when I was an older MFA student at Sarah Lawrence College and she was my teacher. Later we became friends, later still colleagues. Over the twenty-three years we knew each other she was always, even in her last illness, a mentor, someone from whom I never stopped learning. She was also the hub of our small poetry group that met haphazardly from approximately 2004 till 2019. Her loss left me wondering if I would be able to write without her.

It was Jean who began to gather a small group of us to work on poems together. She invited Joan Larkin and me in the beginning. Later, Jan Heller Levi joined us until she moved to Switzerland, and for a short time Jane Mead, whose death preceded Jean's. This group was essential to us, a great nourishment and a place to try out new work. In the last couple of years of Jean's life, as her dementia became more pronounced, I started helping her keep track of her work.

Luckily Jean also had an assistant, Holli Carrell, who helped her by typing some of the new work into a computer file (Jean's own versions were handwritten and/

or typed on a typewriter). Between Holli and me, we had various renderings of new poems: some seemingly finished, others I wasn't sure about. There were also poems that had already been published.

At the last meeting Jean, Joan, and I had together, Jean was stuck on a poem whose title she'd had in her mind for several months. She kept coming back to "Yeats' Stance" but couldn't finish the poem. Despite her illness, Jean was utterly happy talking about poems. She could still focus on poetry if we were together, and still even critique us. She was almost herself in those moments. Speaking about poems, her face would light up and she was our Jean again.

At that meeting when she began to talk about "Yeats' Stance" we wrote down what she said. Later, I went over it with her carefully and she lineated and corrected what didn't feel right to her. "Yeats' Stance" was the last poem she wrote. Interestingly it spoke of her beginnings as a poet, a sense of not feeling welcomed into that male world, Yeats' tower, her experience of *"you are not allowed here."* Despite feeling that she was an outsider in those early years, Jean had managed, over her lifetime, to create a body of extraordinary work. Not a tower exactly, something closer to the earth, maybe unbound by walls, and certainly welcoming.

In January of 2020, before COVID forced us all into isolation here in New York City, Jean and I met and finalized her poems. All edits to her work came from her—I asked questions, some were minor, like spacing or punctuation, and some more complex—but she made all the decisions herself. We laughed a lot. Jean had such a wonderful laugh. I read her poems to her, and she would ask me, *"Did I write that?"*

"You did," I'd answer. She would be so delighted. She would tilt her head and smile, *"Do you think they could ever be in a book?"*

—ANNE MARIE MACARI, SEPTEMBER 2022

New Poems

2016–2020

Light Me Down

Light me down to the long meadow
to where the new snow taps on the fallen snow
with the fingers of the lost tribe.

Who would want us to listen?
Someone does want it:

      Mother of snow
smoking your cigarette ration, your dark
lipstick mouthprint hungry

for the frail paper,
long after the war was over.

The Ring

I wear this ring
I bought before we met—
it's too big,
so I wear it on my thumb.
Away from you,
I look at it more now,
when I go to sleep:

five animals, on a blue ground
with stars—giraffe, elephant,
lion, butterfly, lizard—
then twilight, more stars

Now I lost it.
Now a plain copper one now.
Element.

Now I lost that too.
Here, silver, healing silver. Come.
Holding all colors to you.

To My Teacher

My first own half-grown tenderness
out in the world—you teaching us
Beowulf, World War II, the army, Gertrude Stein,
already a lifetime-full of the meaning of things—
Still now, my second father, gone ahead,
I talk to you. I can't hear your words yet,
but your voice like one of the trees
still around your old GI Bill house: Beowulf poet,
do people meet again? In our same old clothes?
or light?

Thirst

In my first hour, the thirst was for air,
then for my mother, then
existence—
who could I look to be?

—From our first walk alone,
when you're away
or I'm away
I thirst to walk with you
neverleaving.   And blackbird, fly

in the after time.

Image:

women
dressed
in black
in a line
walking, the
third one
with a black
mask over
her eyes
because
she won't see

take
the children!
the man in the tree
is saying
everyone sees things differently

Trust me

with this dear one you hold
& hear & touch

trust me
in your dream

& waking

Pneumonia, January

I dreamed two nights ago
someone said
"I just wanted to ask you
if you were going to go away
different from us."

Dear Adrienne

Remember we sat by your window and smoked,
and read our poems to each other, we

talked about our children, poetry, money, work, race,
home, everything, movies, women's lives,
men, poetry, sex, race, Vietnam,
Berkeley, teaching, women's lives, Dickinson.

Then when you visited me
in Ireland, & we read our poems to each other,
I started breathing again, free from the will
to dominate my own soul.

Last summer, that night at the back of Poets House
at the launch of your last book,
I think you would have liked
the planes going over in the blue light—and the way
Yusef talked about you in the old days—

Adrienne,
the government back here is death to the living,
the earth is in its hands. Talk to me,
tell me the mysteries.

Yeats' Stance

When I was about twenty I went by myself
up into the tower   the holy place
and never questioned it, but felt
I could never be *of* it.

You could feel it in the air
this power

like being shown another planet
and not sure I'd ever come back
from this world of gods who were men.

In these lonely steps I took
there was no one to help me.

You are not allowed here.

The look of the stone the sound
of the stone it's all

go away.

The Teacher

In the library
light drifts across the ceiling

as if we are under water
these years ago

whoever it was approached you,
you lightened the comer:

you holding onto the front of my coat
with both hands, the last time I saw you

the change in your red lips—heart attack,
they said.

                  me? everyone is ok here.

                  I miss you, them too.
It seemed you pulled me out of the ground.

New Poems (2016–2020) | 11

The Cricket

In this little borrowed
wooden house in January,

down on the field-colored rug
I came across a cricket
close to death, or sleeping.
Not breathing, that I could see.

Out walking, I saw a skull of snow,
and a snow-frog listening.
                              Back in the house,
my cricket, your heart has stopped.
Would you like snow over you?
Or be in here together, by the hearth.

But now your body is fallen in pieces around you.
Help me find a leaf for you to lie on, another
to cover you.

Sparrow

What do I want here
Who am I here for   —It seems
—to write to you God,
help me now, your eye is on the sparrow and
I'd die if it is not.

Sparrow my baby died of an abortion.
And I near died. But then they
drove me in a car and caved me back.

My whole life I love you Sparrow,
my whole life—cave me back.

Trust

Our great-aunt Frances's look, trust,

a mare over the half-door
of her stall—

When she was dying
in the thin gray hospital,
her beautiful eyes closed,
a little lick of her dry lips—

In a Diner

I sit across from him—

That I know him.
That I am beginning to know him.

I – half-open:
He sees – what does a half-open
half-palomino see?

To see that.
A voice? A hand?

Not make any sudden movements.

Not lie.
Not leave.

The "thou" is holding up the lit snow.

For Tomas Tranströmer & Max Ritvo

"Come, lonesome one, to the lonesome"
—St. Symeon, the New Theologian, addressing his God.

I looked,
and there he was, my older brother,
my guide to the underworld.
His eyes were kind. He said,
"Here, take my hand, we cross here..."

It was the little blue restaurant.

He was the Swedish poet.
He jumped up over the back of the chair
and sat down right next to Max.
And Max said, "Come, lonesome one,
to the lonesome."

February, 2017

Dear life,
Planes are flying in low
over New Hampshire
under the republic's hysteric
razor cut voice.
Life,
follow the deer
into the woods   learn how to eat
the winter grass under the snow
like your ancestors did—
A little more time

dear life

The Longing

The longing is gone to know you, God
—I know your silence
in the dropped branches,
the lost hands, the lost ship's
voices.

Why I want to talk to you is
I want to die
instead of my young friend.

I know your silence, God,
I have sometimes almost
come to rest with it.
The silence of women.

The 40's

Out the window
there was a linden tree.
Our father was in the war. He sent
censored letters from the Pacific.

Fear and tight cheer in the house,
Roosevelt's faraway voice on the radio at night,
Churchill in the newsreels, Saturdays
with him with Stalin & de Gaulle, announcers' calm voices
over films of the trains, the children, the guards in the camps,
the cold, the hunger. Executions. Our mother
scared to be so blessed.

Poem with a Line from Ko Un

All this from the world,
from the kindness of people,
to the tea in this cup,

—most dear is the silence
the rain   the touch

the touch of your voice in my body
leaving all words behind.

Dear Merton's God

We stand here like trees in the night,
I know you for your words
in the loud silence, your words listen,
they make room for a stranger,
for the dead & the living, the child

We stand here like trees in the night, dear Merton's God,
you throw yourself at us, I know you
for your words in body, in sign language,
I throw myself at you, God, God
you run after people, talking,

people on bicycles, pushing wheelbarrows,
baby carriages, hospital carts, you make room
—with me, you were quiet, you sent it,
or I couldn't have heard it,
sent the warmth deep around my head
like a headband, only inside.

In Ireland

You wanted to see Achill Island
so I drove you there
in the rickety car
slow over the Achill roads.

Later, you called to say you dreamed
I was driving you in that car
up to the passage graves, Carrowkeel,
"the narrow quarter," and you felt safe.

"Safe"—did we not both remember then
the country road we were both once driven over
dangerously   by a soul in danger
—You had cried "Stop."

At the last
the soul couldn't stop.

In China

We are seated on a wide stage. In the bright-lit
auditorium, a PA pronounces the directions in English:
"You are poets. Take off your masks."

A young man stands up & says, in English,
"I come from a small mountain village.
I am studying art. I want to ask,
What is beauty? What to pursue?"

I take off my mask.
What is my love?
with its old hard-beating erotic lungs—
What is my soul,
if it has lost its words?
But it never had its words.
Maybe another look, or step,
or water step or air—

For a friend who died young

Who is my lord?

The bark of the birch tree is

my lord,
the sap of the young tree;

the leap of his voice
in the new branches—

friend,
let me in—

"Regard all dharmas as dreams"

You waking to me
me waking to you
now never not woken

New Poems (2016–2020) | **25**

For Monty

Away, I dream
I see you walking up the block
—the kindest sight on earth

A minute of silence for C.D. Wright

The prophets shade their eyes,
a deer bends his head to a spring,
—C.D. looks back out from a frame of sun and wood.

New Poems (2016–2020) | **27**

The Prison

The gray slate roof for hair,
the six eye-windows,
red bricks for the body, &
God's earth & river floor

—the round black window,
where she looked out,
put her hand up to say *Stop*—

After Fernando Traverso

NI UNO, NI OTRO
NOSOTROS
the rubbed heart
the black bicycle
stenciled on the wall

13/8/93
LORE TE AMO
—the awkward-leaning phone poles,
old men and women resting back
against the sky in blue chairs,

—some sort of opening, like the dream
last night, with you still living—
did you make the dream-opening? or who?
I will carry you. Your happiness.
I am coming.

To who I do know.   *Te amo*.
This happiness.   Old life,
I'm glad, all my rubbed life
I was found,
I was written on a wall in air.

New Poems (2016–2020) | **29**

Here

Sometimes
even as I touch you here
I hear whatever
I could never hear or know
away from you.

I hear what we are meant for
outside this room.

A question lies on my bed—
                    can you tell me?
What is it for the others...
I hear what I could never know

Outside this room   or night

Dream Barker

1965

Dream Barker (1965) | 33

First Love

How deep we met in the sea, my love,
My double, my Siamese heart, my whiskery,
Fish-belly, glue-eyed prince, my dearest black nudge,
How flat and reflective my eye reflecting you
Blue, gorgeous in the weaving grasses
I wound round for your crown, how I loved your touch
On my fair, speckled breast, or was it my own turning;
How nobly you spilled yourself across my trembling
Darlings: or was that the pull of the moon,
It was all so dark, and you were green in my eye,
Green above and green below, all dark,
And not a living soul in the parish
Saw you go, hélas!
Gone your feathery nuzzle, or was it mine,
Gone your serpentine
Smile wherein I saw my maidenhood smile,
Gone, gone all your brackish shine,
Your hidden curl, your abandoned kill,
Aping the man, liebchen! my angel, my own!
How deep we met, how dark,
How wet! before the world began.

For a Woman Dead at Thirty

No one ever talked like that before, like your
Last white rush in the still light of your
Last, bungled fever: no one will any more.

Now we breathe easier: Love,
Released from itself, blows words of love all over,
Now your hands are crossed down there.

We wanted your whole body behind glass,
And you left just half a footprint,
Half-smiling.

All night, driving,
I wanted to know:
At the turn of light that somewhere
Must still be cock's crow

You smiled slantwise in the side mirror,
Six months dead: *here's Romance:*
You wanted to know.

You Never, you blazing
Negative, o you wavering light in water,
Water I stir up with a stick: wavering rot,

O my sister!
          even if I'd known,
All I could have said was that I know.

Miles from Home

Grown, and miles from home, why do I shy
From every anonymous door-slam or dull eye?
The giant-step, the yawn
That streaked my dreams twenty years ago are gone:
The hero and nurse, the smashing Rubens hoof
And fist, the witch who rode my bedroom roof
And made my finger bleed, after all are man and wife
Whose mortal ribs I cracked to water my life,
Whose eyes I weighted keeping my late hours,
Loving my boys, chain-smoking in late, dead bars,
Watching the first light pickle Storrow Drive.

Why did I need that empty space to live?
The hand in the dark was my own, God knows whose cars.

The clay gods lean, and cast shadows under the stars,
Enjoying the blameless flowers on their Boston roof.
The watering-can's bland nozzle gleams like a hoof.

To Salter's Point

Frances Wadsworth Valentine
1880-1959

Here in Framingham, black, unlikely
Wheel spoking into mild Republican townships,
I have come to where the world drops off
Into an emptiness that cannot bear
Or lacks the center to compel
The barest sparrow feather's falling.
Maybe our mortal calling
Is, after all, to fall
Regarded by some most tender care:
But here, the air
Has grown too thin: the world drops off
That could imagine Heaven, or so much care.

Framingham is building. The savage ring
And shake of the drill turn up your morphined sleep.
I fall, still in earth's monstrous pull,
To kiss your hands, your planeless face.
Oh, you are right
Not to know your death-bed's place;
To wander in your drugs from Framingham
To Salter's Point, the long blond beaches where
You and your brothers peeled oranges and swam
While your parents looked on in daguerreotype.

Your iron bedstead there was white like this:
And in this grave, unspeakable night,
Beyond the pull of gravity or care,
You have no place: nor we:

You have taken the summer house, the hedge,
The brook, the dog, our air, our ground down with you,
And all the tall gray children can run
Away from home now and walk forever and ever
And come to nothing but this mouthful of earth,
All endings over.

Lines in Dejection

  for my sister

Remember how we spread our hair on the sea,
Phosphorous fans, the moon's edge crumbling under
Moving pieces of sky? Ghostly weeds loitered
Like misty Thetis's hair, or some sea-monster's
Ancient whiskers, floating around our knees;
Moony children, we drifted, and no god or monster
Could have seemed foreign then to our globe of water.
Remember
Lying like still shells on the glass water?
The paper moon opened, a Japanese water flower
Drifting free of its shell in the bowl of the sky.

Who poured it out? In twenty years
The bay is still in its place, they are still there,
Walking slowly by the water.
Have they been here, all along? Have we?
Back, back, I strike out from the ancestral stare
And now the bowl's shadow composes what I see:
The weeds cradle me and draw me under, under.

Dream Barker (1965) | 37

But there they are, on the pitch-black ocean floor,
Hands out, hair floating: everywhere!
Holding us in their charred arms like water.

Sleep Drops Its Nets

Sleep drops its nets for monsters old as the Flood;
You are not you, no more than I am I;
If our dead fathers walk the wall at night
Our hands when we wake up are white on white
Betraying neither wounds nor blood;
The voice is mist that made us cry.

And then day sweeps the castle dry.

Déjà-vu

No, my father here, as You said,
When I asked him for bread
Didn't refuse me; but the bread was green;
And now You!
Now I'm dry and cold,
Chattering in the corner of the greenhouse,
Now You let me know it was always You,
That déja-vu
Tilt of the sunlight on the floor,
That silence at the door!
I'd laugh, but I never, never loved You,
And here I am dead,
My Midas teeth on edge, green
Jade on jade.

Sunset at Wellfleet

A spit of sky, awash with Venetian gold
Hangs over the Congregational bell-tower, where
Last night the Northern Lights sifted their fire,
Shot through with the airless dark, romantic and cold.
The sun doesn't move, but suddenly is gone,
The cloudy tide goes out, and leaves a ring.
Easy to die: we knew it all along:
Knee-high to the dark as of old:
These words I tell you smoking in my eye:
The tree-frog is the tree-frog. The sky is the sky.
The rattling bay runs night and day *I, I, I,*
Over and over, turning on itself: there,
Where it curls on emptiness: there I sing.

Asleep over Lines from Willa Cather

Now I lay me desolate to sleep
Cold in the sound of the underground flood,
Brushed in half-sleep by the phantom plant
Pressed in the book by my bed
Blue green leaves, large and coarse-toothed . . .
With big white blossoms like Easter lilies . . .
Latour recognized the noxious datura.
In its dead shade I lay me down to sleep.

The reins inside my head that hold my hope
When it leaps, in waking life, fall slack,
And, beyond the world of falling things,
With flesh like air, and an assumed agreement
Between my body and the way it takes,
I walk aimlessly by a green and perfect river.

Dream Barker (1965) | 39

The garden is here, as I knew it would be;
The garden imagined through oblique windows in paintings,
Earth's lost plantation, waiting for all, all,
All to be well: the fountain translates the sun.
I do not see but know God follows me,
And I follow, without fear of madness,
Paths and turnings that are both wild and formal,
Of all colors or none, tiger-lily and rock,
Pools dead with the weight of fallen leaves, and falls,
Follow after him I love, who waits in the garden.

Mercy, Pity, Fear and Shame
Spring in this garden, for it is earth's.
My body is not air, it casts a shadow.
At the next turning I come upon him I love
Waiting by the tree from my childhood that drops
White petals that hugely snow on the whitening ground.
He takes my arm and we walk a little way
Away from the tree towards the shining river
Running clear green through the garden.

The allegorists' arrow has me struck down.
I freeze in the noise of the flood.
When my love bends to speak, it is a language
I do not know: I answer and have no voice,
I am deaf, I am blind, I reach out to touch his face
And touch a spot of spittled clay, my eye,
Hiding the garden, the river, the tree.

Cambridge by Night

Down the aisles of this dark town
Pass faces and faces I have known
In the green, dog days, I forget their names,
Forget their faces.

Every public place in this city
Is a sideshow of souls sword-swallowing pity:
Father Dog-face barks without a sound,
The penny candles stare me down.

You were so close I could have touched the dead
Childhood in your face,
Left my mother's house a bride
With a light,
Night-light, dawn, to be by your side
All night,
But wanting pity, pity stood
Between us in your face.

Nothing troubles the dark: the last
Tiffany windows are out. Their ghosts
Might be my dutch uncles; pity
It's summer, they're out of the city.

To a Friend

I cannot give you much or ask you much.
Though I shore myself up until we meet,
The words we say are public as the street:
Your body is walled up against my touch.

Our ghosts bob and hug in the air where we meet,
My reason hinges on arcs you draw complete,
And yet you are walled up against my touch.

Your love for me is, in its way, complete,
Like alabaster apples angels eat,
But since it is in this world that we meet
I cannot give you much or ask you much.

Dream Barker (1965) | 41

You go your way, I mine, and when we meet,
Both half-distracted by the smells of the street,
Your body is walled up against my touch.

My body sings at your table, waits on the street
And you pass empty-handed, till when we meet
I have been so far, so deep, so cold, so much,
My hands, my eyes, my tongue are like bark to the touch.

Waiting

Ask, and let your words diminish your asking,
As your journal has diminished your days,
With the next day's vanity drying your blood,
The words you have lost in your notebooks.
Ask—do not be afraid. Praise Him for His silence.

What I love to ask is what I know,
Old thoughts that fit like a boot.
What I would hazard clings in my skull:
Pride intervenes, like an eyelid.

All sound slows down to a monstrous slow repetition,
Your times of reflection become a dark shop-window,
Your face up against your face.
You kneel, you see yourself see yourself kneel,
Revile your own looking down at your looking up;
Before the words form in the back of your head
You have said them over and answered, lives before.
O saints, more rollicking sunbeams, more birds about your heads!
Catherine, more Catherine-wheels!

Sic transit gloria mundi,
The quick flax, the swollen globe of water.

Sic transit John's coronation, mortal in celluloid.
Underground roots and wires burn under us.
John outlives the Journal's 4-color outsize portrait
Suitable for Framing, flapping, no color,
No love, in the rain on the side of the paper-shed.

Into Thy hands, O Lord, I commit my soul.
All Venice is sinking.

Let us dance on the head of a pin
And praise principalities!

Life is a joke and all things show it!
Let us praise the night sounds in Connecticut,
The Czechoslovak's parakeet,
Whistling *Idiot, Idiot!*

The moon's disk singes a bucketing cloud
Lit by the sun lit by a burning sword
Pointing us out of the Garden.

Turn your back on the dark reflecting glass
Fogged up with the breath of old words:

You will not be forgiven if you ignore
The pillar of slow insistent snow
Framing the angel at the door,
Who will not speak and will not go,

Numbering our hairs, our bright blue feathers.

Dream Barker (1965) | 43

Sasha and the Poet

Sasha: I dreamed you and he
Sat under a tree being interviewed
by some invisible personage. You were saying
'They sound strange because they were lonely,
The seventeenth century,
That's why the poets sound strange today:
In the hope of some strange answer.'
Then you sang *'hey nonny, nonny, no'* and cried,
And asked him to finish. *'Quoth the potato-bug,'*
He said, and stood up slowly.
'By Shakespeare.' And walked away.

The Second Dream

We all heard the alarm. The planes were out
And coming, from a friendly country. You, I thought,
Would know what to do. But you said,
'There is nothing to do. Last time
The bodies were charred trees.'

We had so many minutes. The leaves
Over the street left the light silver as dimes.
The children hung around in slow motion, loud,
Liquid as butterflies, with nothing to do.

A Bride's Hours

1. DAWN
I try to hold your face in my mind's million eyes
But nothing hangs together. My spirit lies

Around my will like an extra skin
I cannot fill or shake.
My eyes in Bachrach's rectangle look in.
I, who was once at the core of the world,
Whose childish outline held like a written word,
Am frozen in blur: my body, waiting, pours
Over its centaur dreams, and drowns, and wakes
To terror of man and horse.

2. THE BATH
My sisters walk around touching things, or loll
On the bed with last month's *New Yorkers*. My skin,
Beaded with bath-oil, gleams like a hot-house fake:
My body holds me like an empty bowl.
It is three, it is four, it is time to come in
From thinking about the cake to eat the cake.
My sister's voices whir like cardboard birds
On sticks: married, they flutter and wheel to find
In this misted looking-glass their own lost words,
In the exhaled smoke.
                         There isn't a sound,
Even the shadows compose like waiting wings.
I am the hollow circle closed by the ring.

3. NIGHT
I am thrown open like a child's damp hand
In sleep. You turn your back in sleep, unmanned.
How can I be so light, at the core of things?
My way was long and crooked to your hand!
What could your jeweled glove command
But flight of my stone wings?
Our honeymoon lake, ignoring the lit-up land,
Shows blank Orion where to dip his hand.

Dream Barker (1965) | 45

Afterbirth

I loiter in the eye of the Slough,
Every joint aching for sleep;
The sky, inhumanly deep,
Sarcastically casts back the Slough.

Did my child take breath to cry
At the slick hand that hooked her out,
Or cry to breathe? Or did she lie
Still in her private dark, curled taut

Under her sleep's hobgoblin shout?
Anesthesia blew me out:
I gardened shadows in my lost crib
While they took her from me like a rib.

Swaddled and barred, she curls in sleep
At the dry edge of mortality.
If the sky's side proves too steep
Who will take up the little old lady,

Who will call her by her name
When she's a crumble of bones?
What logos lights the filament of time,
Carbon arc fusing birth-stone to head-stone?

The mud pulls harder: the stepping stones
Shake in front of my swimming eyes.
There dear, there dear, here's a pill:
Sleep, sleep, all will be well:
Lull-lullaby.

Sarah's Christening Day

Our Lord, today is Sarah's christening day.
I wouldn't build the child a house of straw,
Teach her to wait and welcome the holy face
With candles of prayer, or pray, if the wager were all.
But I have never seen or loved the holy face.
I don't believe the half of what I pray.

This world is straw: straw mother, father, friend,
Per omnia saecula saeculorum, amen.
But Lord! it shines, it shines, like light, today.

Tired of London

When you came to town,
Warm bubbling rains came, the teething leaves,
Steaming spring earth, and the touch, small-footed birds;

Reckless colors sifted the closed, dense sky
As we went hand in hand through our larky maze
In the cultivated stubble of Hampstead Heath:

Monkshood, Foxglove, Canterbury Bells
Composed themselves to drink the Bovril air
Thinned by the watery sun.

You, with no sense of giving,
Brought all the dangers I no longer dared;
Netted the wind that roared through my rented bed,

And, poised like Eros over Picadilly,
Were always there.
I cannot find the words to leave you with.

Dream Barker (1965) | 47

This way love's conversation, the body and mind of it, goes
On after love: we shall come to call this love,
And this roar in our ears which before very long
We become, we shall call our song.

Cambridge,
April 27, 1957

Your letter made me see myself grown old
With only the past's poor wing-dust shadows to hold,
Dressed in violet hand-me-downs, half-asleep, only half,
Queer as nines in the violet dust of my mind,
Leaning in some sloping attic, like this one where I write
You all night,
The wet, metaphorical Cambridge wind
Sorry on the skylight.
                            The New England landscape goes
Like money: but here on Agassiz Walk we save
Everything we have
Under Great-Aunt Georgie's georgian bed;
A knot garden roots through Great-Aunt Georgie's toes
Three floors below: when summer comes, God knows
We'll dry the herbs Aunt Georgie grows:
Who knows, who knows
What goes on in her head.

I read Thoreau myself, I listen for Thoreau
Up here; wonder if there's a burial mound
Anywhere for Henry: PAX, AETAT.
45. Quiet Desperation. REQUIESCAT,

Ducky: one of these nice days
My niece, the one with one glass eye,
Is driving me out to Walden Pond:
Cross my heart, I hope to die.

New York,
April 27, 1962

When we get old, they say, we'll remember
Things that had sunk below the mind's waking reach
In our distracted years; someday, knees blanketed, I will reach out
To touch your face, your brown hair.

Remember now thy Creator in the days of thy youth.
I rest, tending children, in hollow, light rooms,
Sleep in their milky fingers, after years
Howling up on the tiles while my goblins threw their shoes.

The child I carry lies alone:
Which hag did we not invite to its conception?
I cat-nap, remembering the tiles.

And you?
Steps on the sidewalk outside my barred New York windows
Land on the cracks, let out the bears,
Loose them on the child who is not there;
Footsteps that gleam in their echo of SS men's heels
Off-stage in my first movies: approaching the door.
We huddle inside and wake to remember it's Peace.
Peace. But you are not here, nor are you dead.

No-one forgot my birthday. Twenty-eight.
How shall we celebrate?
Fetch my blanket, dearest, there's something in the air,
Dark, quick, quicksilver, dark eyes, brown hair,
Bringing all the presents: someone is coming late:
The babies cry, the bell rings in thin air.

Dream Barker (1965) | 49

September 1963

We've been at home four years, in a kind of peace,
A kind of kingdom: brushing our yellow hair
At the tower's small window,
Playing hop-scotch on the grass.

With twenty other Gullivers
I hover at the door,
Watch you shy through this riddle of primary colors,
The howling razzle-dazzle of your peers.

Tears, stay with me, stay with me, tears.
Dearest, go: this is what
School is, what the world is.
Have I sewed my hands to yours?

Five minutes later in the eye of God
You and Kate and Jeremy are dancing.

Glad, derelict, I find a park bench, read
Birmingham. Birmingham. Birmingham.
White tears on a white ground,
White world going on, white hand in hand,
World without end.

Riverside

Now, with March forcing our brittle spines like first childbirth,
Scattering our notes, making the house cold inside,
Riverside Park turns up its vestiges of God
Where bare-faced boys in their sweat-suits lope through the last light
Alongside long-haired girls, half-tree,
And every dog is a brother, or half-brother,

50 | *Light Me Down: The New & Collected Poems of Jean Valentine*

And the cold-war babies span their tender fists,
198?, to net the sun
Spun gold in these thousand pigeon brown windows
Then OUT in a mushroom of neon over Hoboken:
And I, like you, am I, in the eyes of the angels.

Winter was the time for the kind of death we enjoyed:
Then the crust of the earth was something arbitrary;
Branches roots, the sky a vein of tin,
Leaves rose, smoke fell, all the old ladies
Waiting on the benches grew beards waiting.
We talked on the phone, napped, grew white and dry
And leapt at misunderstanding, forcing the news
Every day, the news of the end of love
From the earth's four corners: then left home in the dark,
Dropping pebbles behind us, came
Into the cold: tears from the cold
Stood in our eyes like tears.

Now, with March,
The woods begin to move, and I
Hold your body in my mind, and see
In each man here a mooning orphan boy,
In every long-haired girl a bearded lady,
In every dog the green part of my mind.
That couple stops: tenderly
He carves their initials in her bright green bark.
She takes a child, the moon climbs one slow step
And stands alone; and I
Keep in and chip in my sleep at winter's bone.

For Teed

April 6th: the country thaws and drips,
The worm turns under the town,

Under the world: the freed earth gapes
In wily Ulysses' lips,
The dust of his wrist rests
In caves that were Penelope's breasts,
Even the dog is gone
White-eyed to Acheron:
No Elizabeth, no Jack
Has come back.
Here lies Teed.
Surviving her are

God, can you hear her
Sing? how earth is freed
Of Teed's winter,
Morphine, flowers
Curled on the radiator,
Freed of her visiting hours,
The night sounds of St. Luke's,
Of her fortune-cookie body, freed
Of the whole table reading *cancer*.
The needle trembles, breaks!
Her face swells: can you hear?
Freed of her! of her!

My Grandmother's Watch

Your first child was my father,
Old *muti* of Buffalo, little old child heiress,
My black-eyed baby, chain-smoking gold-
Tipped English Ovals in Heaven: your brassy
Churchillian French reduced us all to *mots*,
Even from the hardly troubled, lavendered sheets of your deathbed.

I wear your coin-thin red gold watch now, Momma,
Its face benign as the Archduke's, and think of your hours,

And what has gone between us, what is ours.
Tonight, for instance: my tongue is thick with longing:
When the children's visit was over, the cake cleared away,
What possessed your mahogany beasts to stay?

On the night of my eighteenth birthday
You made me a toast, saying I
Was not only good at school, but musical!
Pink-cheeked, black-hearted, shy,
I couldn't even look you in the eye:
They cleared the cake away.

The insanely steady minute-hand sweeps round,
The hours go by. Somebody said
His Viennese grandfather
Sold him his watch on his deathbed.
Did you too?

What can I do?

O Momma, what can I
Do with this gold and crystal that goes by?

The Beast with Two Backs

Excursion: a night, two days
Away from home and neighborhood,
Double-locked doors, mirror-
Backed peep-holes: the neighbors.

How big they've grown, the children!
Make them walk! It's not good,
A woman, the insides! Daughters,
You'll always have them; five sons,

Dream Barker (1965) | 53

One's in Teaneck. Make her walk!
You'll break your mother's back!

The boat: by Christ, an excursion.
Every man has seven wives, each wife
Has seven children, each child has seven guns.
The ladies change, they do change, in the Ladies'
Room: they wink, they shrug, they look over their backs
At their colorful tails. I look at my toes
In the stall where the toilet roils with the white Atlantic.

Over the Times we talk about Ho,
Allen Dulles, Malcolm X: take up our Signet Classics.
Someone across the way from us is reading *The Guermantes' Way*,
Who smiles. It is a long trip to our island,

Seven years already,
Longer than anyone ever would have thought.
We buy beer; I'd like
A colorful tail like that.

On our island we walk, eat, lie,
Drink, walk, analyze, analyze.
This moon we do not like we'll like
Remembering, and know it.
Do we trust ourselves more this morning?
Today we can stay in bed all day. Ah, love,

The soap, Irina! You have no soap! The sheets,
Irina, in Six! Knock knock.

Knock. We give it up, we are married
Seven years, we can smile with the backs of our heads:
The two-backed beast is wild,
We let him go.
                    He said. She said.
He said.

54 | *Light Me Down: The New & Collected Poems of Jean Valentine*

                We turn our backs
For home.
                On the wall it said "For Fire:
Continuous ringing of bell and call of FIRE."

The Little Flower

I thank God, I have never taken to drinking, as many I know have, I
    have never done that and my children should be thankful but they
    are not, I have not been that kind,
I say my prayers every night,
Lots of them do and with less reason, I did once but put it from me,
and with all the shocks I have had to bear, such shocks in those ter-
rible years, you do not know, my father, my father was a mean man,
Given to giving nicknames,
He called me Susan B. Anthony because I was so strong I guess, I have
    never given way as others would have done, he called your aunt
    Bunny because when her first two teeth came in he said *she looks*
    just like a bunny, she did look just like a bunny, *we will call her*
    Bunny and so she is to this day I am eighty-three she must be
    eighty, strange she was always jealous of my looks Bun was, I was
    tall and slim
And very beautiful they all said so,
And she thought I had all the looks always was a jealous kind of per-
    son but you know she was very lovely too, I was jealous of her too,
    isn't that funny I always thought Bun had such nice feet and I al-
    ways thought my feet were ugly isn't that funny, the things you will
    get into your head, feet
It hasn't all been roses,
My mother was a Ross a Ross from Scotland, they were a noble clan,
    your mother sent me a postcard once of the Ross castle, I have it
    somewhere in these suitcases, it's in the north
Oh I must set my things in order
I must have help to set my things in order, so many papers, no one

will come and soon I will be gone and then who will, No now we
will talk it is so good, to have someone to talk to, is that chair all
right for you not in a draft, this room has a terrible draft you have
beautiful eyes,
A little like mine oh when I was younger
You have always been a good child and you know you get funny all
alone in a room I hope I have never complained but you get and at
my age, no one understands what it is like to be old, does my mind
wander, that is what I
I forget things
Words do not come to my mind, my mother was a Ross from Scot-
land, they were a noble clan, she used to tell such wonderful stories
and sing us the old songs she would go on with those stories and
songs the children loved her, she came and visited us often and
stayed weeks and weeks, she was always there if I were sick, I hope
she always knew she had a home with us and I was sick so much
with the climate what it was and the miscarriages and the babies,
and she always came to be a comfort to me, but then she died,
What it is like
He had died long before that, there is a place for Bun and a place for
me with them in the plot in Minneapolis, I don't care about cre-
mation it seems the cleanest thing you don't mind talking about
these things do you, neither do I some people do but I don't mind
talking about these things at all, look at my teeth, if I do not get to
the dentist, but I cannot even get dressed, just to get dressed but I
get so dizzy, when I stand I am so afraid of falling again, will you
look at my teeth, I try not to smile so as to show them, I always
had beautiful teeth
It seems the cleanest thing
Bunny has written me a long letter about it, she's going to be cre-
mated, Henry was too, you pack a bag with the clothes you want
to go in and if you go in winter like her Henry did, and a godsend,
they wait till Spring to put you in the ground, Henry's there, no I
don't mind about cremation as long as they make sure I'm good
and dead first, ha, ha,
Look at my teeth
The children loved her, she would tell them those stories over and

over, no I don't remember any of them, not one, and the children
   don't any more, I asked Louise and she said, No Mother, I like to
   tell you these things because soon I will be gone and then no one
   will remember all this
My father
There do you hear her, there she goes, eight or ten hours a day some
   days, they say she is an opera singer, it goes right through my
   spine, we would always come to New York here for the opera sea-
   son, we always took the same suite at the Plaza Hotel, the manager
   was a very fine gentleman, he always said to me, Mrs. Haran, your
   children are the best behaved children who have ever visited us
   here at the Plaza Hotel, and they were, so quiet
They all said so
Your grandfather used to love the operas and then we always had sea-
   son tickets for the Chicago Symphony, I would take the children
   every Friday afternoon, do you hear her, I have sent a note to the
   desk but they say there is nothing they can do, I must take another
   room, on another floor, another hotel
Just to get dressed
Your mother always had a gift for music, she had lessons from the age
   of five with the best piano teacher in the city, but no when she
   married him she let it go, I told her, you will be sorry Louise, if
   you have music you will always have that whatever comes, like
   books, my children all loved books if you give children the love of
   books they will always have that whatever comes, will you listen to
   that woman, I have told them at least let her be still Sundays, at
   least let me have peace Sundays but you know they are all Jewish
   people in this hotel
Not that I
Not that I have anything against Jewish people if you like them I hope
   I am not so narrow, it is all knishes, what are they, and lox and the
   good Lord knows what on the menu, I cannot eat it, Ramon my
   waiter says ¡Ah Mrs. Haran you did not eat! they all loved reading,
   if I could only read but it hurts my eyes so
Even the Tribune
With everything else I had to bear there were always books, I used to
   read a book a day, oh yes and magazines, Edward used to tease me

Dream Barker (1965) | 57

for taking the Post but I have always said there are lots of fine arti-
cles in the Post I still take it but now I can hardly read the Tribune,
Dr. Giroux wants me to see an ophthalmologist
Just to get dressed
Edward your uncle Edward was a great reader, he was always reading,
he always said he loved to read with me there in the room, we al-
ways read together like that when he was little, those were bad
years, that was when it was just beginning, he was reading to him-
self at three years, his teachers always told me, Eddie has a wonder-
ful mind, they called him Eddie, I was always with him when he
was little, that was when your grandfather began to take too much,
then I was so ill and Edward would always come in and sit by me,
I was in bed so much, months at a time, Edward would say
Mother shall I sit with you a while, he was always considerate that
way most children are not you know, Edward was
To be a comfort
They were seven brothers the children's uncle Jack was first, the mon-
signor, then your grandfather, and the others were all born over
here, well they scattered around the middle west, mostly farming
and such, your grandfather was the only one of them who ever
made his way, and Jack, one went to California I think, oh the Lord
knows where they all are now living or dead, they all blamed me
Listen to her
We had an audience with the Pope did I ever tell you that I like to tell
you these things, Pope Pius X, he was a very charming man,
charming, a gentleman I shall never forget it, a private audience,
no he spoke English, your uncle Jack was at the American College,
he arranged it all, no I went to the Church long before I ever met
your grandfather I was still at home well it seemed to draw me in I
don't know why, my father said it was just like me, *The Little
Flower* he called me
A religious man, they were all religious men
I have always held that your church doesn't matter as long as you live
right you must give the children some faith to stand by them when
their troubles come, it doesn't matter what church I hope I am not
so narrow, but it breaks my heart to see Billy and her raising those
children without anything, he always went to the best Catholic

schools, I gave him that, and how can he stand by and watch her
raise those children with nothing, and how can she let him get
so heavy
It's the drinking
I'm sorry, I hope I've always been good to her the same as I am with
all of you yet she never brings them, they are my grandchildren
and I never see them, they do not know me, they lose that you
know, they will never have those memories, it is nice to have a
sense of family
They all blamed me
We went down, Jack had a summer place at that castle Gandolfo you
know, very nice, outside Rome, it was hot, I remember I was faint
do you hear her ah-ah-ah-ah, no no coffee for me I can't take it,
my lower intestine, well, and then I get so terribly dizzy, Dr. Giroux
has given me pills for it but I don't like to take them, just some ice
water is all, there in that green bottle, Tipperary was where they
came from but they were originally Normans
Normans who came over from France
Jack was good to us at first, for a while, at the beginning he would
take his dinner with us every night, so as to keep the idea of a fam-
ily for the children, he cared a lot for that, priests do they don't
know, that was when it was beginning with your grandfather, the
stocks dropping and his partner and all and the never coming home
The children never knew
I spared them that, and the miscarriages, it was not so easy in those
days to have a baby, you girls today, and my back was never strong
to carry them, six months in bed before Billy, and then the broth-
ers tried to get me to have him back, they all blamed me
Normans
I was never off a penny in my books when I was spending thousands
of dollars managing Astor Street and now I'm always so confused
that is what terrifies me, my checkbook is in such a state and no
one, I ask Billy but he never comes, I guess she won't let him away,
I don't think much of a person like that, I like to keep two thou-
sand dollars margin in case I have to go to the hospital or so when
I go it will, but it's under that now I don't know how much and I
make mistakes in my arithmetic, and then these medicines, forty

dollars, fifty dollars, I feel awful, the children do not understand or
they would not be so
What it is like
None of you, but you are a good child, I always had a special place in
my heart even when you were little, of course I loved you all, and I
worry so about you, when you get old you worry a lot, there's some
nice cake in there on the shelf chocolate the kind you like, I got it
in last week expecting you, oh I know how much you have to do at
home, I hope you're through having children now, two is a nice
family plenty these days, you know just a phone call would mean a
lot when you have a minute
The children do not know
I hate to call you I know how busy you are, I hope I haven't asked
much of my family, I know you're all caught up in your own life
the family and all, you look tired, I loved my children I hope I
loved my children
None of you
I hope I was good to him, everything a wife should be, he was proud
of me, all my clothes were made specially for me, and I was never
off a penny in my books and they all loved to come to Astor Street,
I remember Mr. Fairbank a millionaire there, he used to always
come and he could have had anything in the world, he loved to
come to us, he said, Nelly I feel at home here, a charming man, a
very old family, no airs, no I never turned him away while he was
well, I was everything a wife should be, it wasn't easy but men are
that way and I hope I never let him know while he was well
Anything in the world
He used to say, Nelly, you make me feel very grateful, and he tried to
be very considerate that way while he was well, not all men do, you
know, he did try
Music whatever comes
What could I do, it was such a shock, the money, and then him never
coming home and the drinking, I had the children to think of,
they never knew, Jack tried to help him, first talking himself then
the doctors, but nothing helped, he got worse, worse, he had had
so much, risen from nothing himself, and he became deluded after
the drop, losing more and more, he was on the telephone talking

business as if he were still what he had been, then I had to call
back, I was so ashamed, and explain he was not well, everyone was
very kind, I couldn't go out of the house
I had the children to think of
I kept everything just as it had been for them, Dr. Lapham their doc-
tor, he was a world-famous pediatrician, he died of pneumonia in
Boston, he had called on me the day before he went just to see
how we were getting along, he said, Mrs. Haran try to do for the
children just as you would have done, and I did, Billy went to
Canterbury and Harvard, Louise had a beautiful debut, I always
had all her clothes made specially for her and there wasn't a better
dressed girl her year, or a prettier, it wasn't as if we had a lot
Dr. Lapham
But I always remembered what Dr. Lapham had said, many women
would not have done it that way for their children, I should have
thought of my own old age
Dr. Lapham
They all blamed me when he was put in the mental home, it was the
best state institution in the middle west, I had the children to
think of, they said there was money enough for private care but I
knew what there was and I knew he couldn't be helped, we had
spoken to the best doctors in Chicago, do you know what the pri-
vate places cost, and he lived, he lived for years and years, he only
died three years ago, there wasn't that kind of money for him, look
how I've had to manage all these years, and I had to do for the
children it would all have gone, what would I have done, no he
hadn't lost much yet but he would have if he'd gone on, I had to
save what I could
I knew
They kept trying to get him away, one Christmas they got him out, a
trick, and brought him down to Minneapolis, it was Christmas
night, so cold, and we had to take him back, he was not respon-
sible then for what he said, he was ill the doctors could not do any-
thing for him, the money was gone, all but what I had managed to
keep away, I had the children to think of, and myself
He was not responsible then
Then later Billy and your mother brought him east to another state

home, New York State, up here, they said it was a better place, no
they never visited him, he did not know them anymore they said,
that was when they were grown of course when they were young
they never knew
They all blamed me
Dr. Lapham did not blame me, I asked him, in the worst of it, I had
no one to turn to and I asked him and he said, it is very hard
Mrs. Haran, he understood and Edward understood he was older
than the others and I used to talk to him I had no one, oh of
course I didn't tell him the truth, but he was with me and that was
a comfort, Bun came but she did not understand ever, she always
thought he could be helped by the doctors, she never understood
They all blamed me
We didn't see her for a long while and then we didn't talk about it any
more, but I knew she blamed me, she used to say, he loves you
Nelly, she never understood he had never loved me never, only the
house and the clothes and that
Edward understood
He was always with me if it hadn't been for Edward there were times I
would have committed suicide, I know it's a terrible thing to say,
but those were terrible years, but for Edward who always under-
stood, and he was always there, later I wanted him to go out and
get a place of his own, make his life away from all my troubles, but
he always said No Mother and he always stayed until he died four
years ago, the night he died his car went over a bridge
It was the eye drops
He'd been reading Stendahl On Love, he was always a great reader,
when he died the doctor came in the middle of the night and gave
me an injection, she was so kind to me that country doctor, she
understood
Edward understood
It is a terrible thing to lose a child, no matter how old they are they are
always your children and you always worry, I gave them every-
thing, and then he died, and the other two never come, what have
done, your mother came when he died to be with me, she
blamed me, I know she blamed me
Never only the house

She did not know how it was with Edward, the drinking and the
trouble, I never told anyone, he needed me, thank God I had the
money to help him out of his trouble, it was always the same, I
was always there
Died, died
I should have thought more of myself, other women would have saved
for themselves, learn from your grandmother
Christmas night
What it is like to be old, and alone, and sick, and I worry so about
money, not about leaving a lot behind, I have done enough I hope,
but I don't know how long I'll last, which will go first, ha, ha, the
money or me
Always the same
Every night when I lie down I think they'll find me in the morning, I
always have the bag ready, that blue one dear you should know,
every night I wash my feet before I get into bed, they never think
what it is like,
The children loved her,
Thousands of dollars, I loved my children, I hope I loved my children,
what have I done that they are strangers to me, sometimes at night
when I can't sleep
Whatever comes
I never sleep till three or four in the morning or five and then at eight
or nine she starts up with her scales sometimes I think I must have
said something or done something to hurt them, something I do
not know, do you know? then I pray
Deliver her soul, O Lord
And that has been a comfort to me these last years, though what the
Lord has done for me I don't know, I hope I've always lived right,
and surely the Lord should not refuse His creatures
And let my cry come unto Thee
Most children are not you know, Edward was, they all blamed me,
always the same, gone, and then no one, look at my teeth, I am
afraid to die, you are young but you know you get afraid
I knew
It's good to talk like this to someone, and then I like to tell you these
things, never, only the house, died, died, died, soon I will be gone
and then no one will remember, there do you hear her, none of you.

Dream Barker (1965) | 63

Sex

All the years waiting, the whole, barren, young
Life long. The gummy yearning
All night long for the far white oval
Moving on the ceiling;
The hand on the head, the hand in hand;
The gummy pages of dirty books by flashlight,
Blank as those damaged classical groins;

Diffusion of leaves on the night sky,
The queer, sublunar walks.
And the words: the lily, the flame, the truelove knot,
Forget-me-not; coming, going,
Having, taking, lying with,
Knowing, dying;
The old king's polar sword,
The wine glass shattered on the stone floor.

And the thing itself not the thing itself,
But a metaphor.

Adam and Eve: Poem on Folded Paper

We dream of saving what
cannot
Can't touch through this glass
pane
Pain that cuts the green world
down
Down, derry down with my true
love
Loving the one human voice we
heard
Heard myself answer in a

64 | *Light Me Down: The New & Collected Poems of Jean Valentine*

dream
Dream now, Adam, and wake to find no
world
The world's a dance of spiders against this
pane
And pain is their condition.

Dream Barker

We met for supper in your flat-bottomed boat.
I got there first: in a white dress: I remember
Wondering if you'd come. Then you shot over the bank,
A Virgilian Jim, and poled us off[1]
To a little sea-food barker's cave you knew.

What'll you have? you said. Eels hung down,
Bamboozled claws hung up from the crackling weeds.
The light was all behind us. To one side
In a dish of ice was a shell shaped like a sand-dollar
But worked with Byzantine blue and gold. *What's that?*

Well, I've never seen it before, you said,
And I don't know how it tastes.
Oh well, said I, *if it's bad,*
I'm not too hungry, are you? We'd have the shell...
I know just how you feel, you said

And asked for it; we held out our hands.
Six Dollars! barked the barker, *For This Beauty!*
We fell down laughing in your flat-bottomed boat,

---

1. The original version of this poem, as first published in 1965, contained harmful language. After careful consideration, the editors made the decision to remove the language. The inclusion of this footnote acknowledges the alteration, seeking to balance the preservation of Valentine's literary scholarship and art with the sensitivity to how it is presented to readers.

Dream Barker (1965) | **65**

And then I woke up: in a white dress:
Dry as a bone on dry land, Jim,
Bone dry, old, in a dry land, Jim, my Jim.

To My Soul

after Hadrian and Ronsard

Scattered milkweed, valentine,
Moonlighting darling, leonine
Host and guest of my chêateau,

Tender, yawning concubine,
Vine of my summer in decline,
Uncut, unribboned mistletoe,

Monstrous footprint in the snow,
Hypnotizing, gemmy toad,
My generations' cameo,

Symplegadês of every road,
Closet bones, unflowered sod,
Laugh, my little nuncio!

Pilgrims

1969

With gratitude
to Mr. Gerald Freund,
and The Rockefeller Foundation;
and to Miss Constance Smith,
and The Radcliffe Institute

ἐγὼ δὲ κῆν' ὄττω
τις ἔραται

"... but I say whatever
one loves, is"
—Sappho

PART I

The Couples

One night they all
found themselves alone,
their first force gone.
No law.

Vacations were no vacation,
nothing came in the mail,
and so on. Everyone
wanted to be good,

no one alive remembered them.

Out of decency no one spoke.
By the time day broke
even the babies were bored with them,
with hunger, and falling;

even you, Prince, gray
around the mouth and tired of calling,
tired of briars, tired of them,
had ridden away.

Fireside

The fox went under the garden
thinking. The watersnake
never moved, or the sun.
—Night, and everyone's straight out

longing; the cat's in the woods,
the children lie loose in stories
tall as this world could
be if we could run for it Lord

Fox. Foxfire will, we thought, out,
you and I, blue glass at the fire-
side side by side,
word for word,
wood for wood,
desire for desire,
nicer than God.

Solomon

Still, gold, open-handed,
sad King Solomon
listened: they started,
weightless, close to his ear,
sweet as bees.

One with light breasts and knees
danced with herself before Solomon,
one stood by with barbarian eyes
mad for Solomon,
one, a child, even touched his face

and he smiled in his clothes,
shut his eyes.

Solomon sat by a white pond
his skin thin gold
and his head down.

Pilgrims (1969) | 73

One stood by with barbarian eyes
mad for Solomon.
She came to his hands,

light, far, anyone
or no one. Solomon
touched her eyes.

                    Too close,
too heavy, the dark
did just what it had promised,

the park turned sharp as it had started:

he closed his hands.

In the Museum

There is a stone
where the Buddha was.
Nothing: air,

one footprint; his chair
a stone.
We stood

back, out of harm;
smiled; right?
went on.

The next room, love,
was funnier: all that love-making
in broad daylight,

and every one of them smiling.
Back where the Buddha was, the stone,
happy as God,

grinned like bone,
love: the air,
asking nothing,

smiled everywhere.

Come.

By the Boat Pond
for S

The newspapers blowing over the street
made her cry, all the birds in New York were crying
because they couldn't speak Greek,

she took nothing with her and went out onto the street.
The day was obscure, one more
lick of the quiet
licking at the door,

her soft black magic,
swallowing him, the children,
the world: leaving, everyone leaving,
all turning angels or nothing,

nothing or swimming like paradise children.

Pilgrims (1969) | **75**

The Summer House

I
She took his hand
so he brought her to his country:
'See it is dry': and

it was a light field, water,
a tree loud as water
in that wind.

—In your country
there is a light field, water.

Your body is in this wind,
I am in your mouth, your hand.

II
There were times
out of time's drag
we'd be without fixed faces
bodies or words; times

held like a feathery scene
on a Quimper plate: v's of quick birds
in their aviary sky, blue flowers
strung all around the dot-faced boy and girl:

all afternoon the sunlight ticked across
sleep, across our borrowed house.

III
The angels we made in the snow
are blown and the shapes at the snows edge
are only themselves again

and we our taller selves
smoke between the house and the woods' edge,
dying to come in or have snow:

—Does he love her? She loves,
he loves, they

love the old stories of the snow
and the look of the house. Together so.

Woods

Dearest darling woodenhead
I love you

I can taste you
in bed laughing

come on Teach I love your
hair

Penseroso,
crab, you angel!

feel me on the palm of your hand?
Look

all the thin trees
are hanging this morning ready to fuzz,

high birds I can't see are whistling,
winter's dripping down

Pilgrims (1969) | 77

faster and faster and
faster. And not to death.

Wait.

Her dream: the child
for M.R

It stared and stared
right through them to the world.

But it better come in said
a quiet man and she said Look
and took it into bed.

They lay closer
in the pale morning. Three flat white ducks
on the wall woke up and took off.

In the morning
he woke them up humming.

Orpheus and Eurydice
> 'What we spent, we had.
> What we had, we have.
> What we lost, we leave.'
> —Epitaph for his wife and himself,
> by the Duke of Devon, twelfth century

I
You. You running across the field.

A hissing second, not a word,
and there it was, our underworld:
behind your face another, and another,
and I

away.

—And you alive: staring,
almost smiling;

hearing them come down, tearing
air from air.

II
'This dark is everywhere'
we said, and called it light,
coming to ourselves.
                    Fear
has at me, dearest. Even this night
drags down. The moon's gone. Someone
shakes an old black camera-cloth
in front of our eyes.
Yours glint like a snowman's eyes.
We just look on, at each other.

What we had, we have. They circle down.
You draw them down like flies.
You laugh, we run
over a red field, turning at the end to blue air,—
you turning, turning again! the river
tossing a shoe up, a handful of hair.

Pilgrims (1969) | 79

Goodbye

after Bella Akhmadulina

And finally I'll say goodbye.
Don't feel you have to love.
I'm chattering, crazy,
or maybe coming into a crazier kind of peace.

How you loved! Your lips just grazing over disaster,
tasting nothing. But that doesn't matter.
How you loved! How you destroyed!
Offhandedly, like a great pale curious boy.

O coldness of failure, cold certainty,
there's no settling with you. The body
wanders around, sees light; sun and moon
shine through the glass pane.

The empty body goes on with its little task.
But the hands fall light and slack,
and like a small flock, sideways,
all sounds and smells graze off away.

Separation

I
OK my child
but not unmake
the smudge of black
under his eyes, their eyes,

or turn it back to the quiet, best
time we sat
in the front room; dumb,
dressed, affectionate.

II
There is fear there, but you know
it's fear. Why,
summer's just going to be starting;
I have work,
I have friends,
I have whatever I had.

I mean to take hold
like a tree. There's tar,
bolts, wires. Leaves.

The trees rattle all around.
Jack and Elizabeth live in a hidden house
and hold hands in it;

they smile at me as if in the past,
as if kindly. O Jack and Elizabeth will you marry
marry you will Elizabeth and Jack o. Jack is

rubbing her back
down in front of the summer fire
her eyes are apple green.

Out of the blue, your face
bent over some book you love.

To bed. Sheet lightning on sheet glass, a morning
enough. Enough
I don't understand:

these wires. The white
wet root here
now. These people's bread.

III
The children make spy-maps of the neighbors for you

and paste leaves on. The river wind blows the leaves,
the neighbors rock on cinders hour to hour,
hot. I watch nights from my sliding corner
out to where you are: the street, where your
back goes walking, talking,
talking. You take daylight,
and the law, the way things tick.
And us, wherever you go, —leaves,
how we float, and stick!

IV
Breaking. I just sit. Well,
I hear noises.

I hope to hear noises, wishes
lip up over the steps all night:

flying fish,
my own breathing.

Without knowing anything,
without money, America,
without leaving,

coming to a new country.
Your two hands,
a few names.

Over and over without a smile
the little walls break up and bleed
pure violence and mend and mend.

Thinking about Cain

> God to Cain: 'and if thou doest not well,
> sin lieth at the door. And unto thee shall be
> his desire, and thou shalt rule over him.'

The first life's blood. Now day
lies at the door, the clocks tick,
the smoky kitten nurses at my salty fingers,
not the best. Six-thirty, time

to get up, to get the children up,
to find the mother,
the father.
In the holes they left. Doors!

Ways open to befriend our friends,
our words, our worst old ways, to learn

to love this circling through and through
the veins of those two that day, *thou*.

Dearest,

      this day broke
at ten degrees. I swim
in bed over some dream sentence lost
at a child's crying: the giant on her wall
tips the room over, back:
I tell her all I know,
the walls will settle, he'll go.

Holding her fingers, I watch the sky rise, white.
The frost makes about the same lines
on the same window as last winter,
quicker, quieter . . . I think how nothing's happened,

how to know
to touch a face to make a line
to break the ice to come in time
into this world, unlikely, small,
bloody, shiny, is all, is God's good will
I think, I turn to you,
and fail, and turn,

as the day widens
and we don't know what to do.

PART II

April

Suppose we are standing together a minute
on the wire floor of a *gaswagen*:
suppose we are in the dark.

It's warm and dry.
We have food.
We aren't in hiding waiting, mostly
we're sitting in our own light rooms.

Come over, bring things: bring
milk, peanut butter,
your pills, your woolens, crayons.

Nuns pray.
Snow. It's dark.
Pray for our friends who died
last year and the year
before and who will die this year.

Let's speak,
as the bees do.

Broken-down Girl

Imagine her quick
who could talk
and cry, still
running, under
the whole sky,
the youngest sister,

who fumbled down
in such sincere pieces.
Silver pieces!
The wind,
the Virginia rain,
touch your face

now none of us
at this table
could, frail
gleam, glass face
without a back,
open book,
telstar.

Pilgrims (1969) | 85

Bin Dream, West Cottage East, D-II

You or I,

sweet Mag, miserable sixteen, paternal,
put the kettle on,
set out three white cups,
and forgot,

the minister edged up sideways
with a certain amount of floor to cross
to the silver sink the radio
the fireplace and the cup,

the sky inched into blue-white milk,
the housemother stood up,
looking at us all, not warmly,
said, *No one*

ate, Mag
put the kettle on

you, your father, your married sister,
or I

Bin Dream #2, Interview with Stravinsky

"Gossip is travel,
and in these times, like travel,
speeded up to the nth degree,
and that's alright,

if you remember of an afternoon
the immeasurable sift

of geological time, the slowness
of say slow snow,

               gossip deriving
from the ancient Aramaic
word, *sari,* or *safari,*

meaning
to travel,
or, to love."

Death House

It was the same kind of night, the light, the coughing,
huge shoes walking, your breathing
through three walls, sleeping into the last things.

In the corner of our grove
the newest one kept on saying
oh, I, oh, I,
Oh him, the guard grinned, going by,
and woke you up. You went ahead.

The guard went ahead.
This is the room, here come the City's dead,
grave sisters, fur-trapping fathers,
mothers still waiting, falling
past my free hands,
and my hands falling.

Pilgrims (1969) | **87**

Archangel

It's dark in here,
your halo looks flat as a plate.
Maybe we're still there. Was that lightning?

You look like a cat when you sleep.
I'm not sleeping. You reading?
I'm looking for this poem,

about a cat—wait a minute—
Go on.
You can read to me all you want.

That time it was lightning.
Is it you? Rolling the green grass back?
I love it when you smile like that.

Is this the white dawn, Angel, in the book?
It's dawn. Look.
Where are they bringing the rock back?

Where are you going?

Half an Hour

Hurt, hurtful, snake-charmed,
struck white together half an hour we tear
through the half-dark after

some sweet core,
under, over gravity,
some white shore . . .

spin, hidden one, *spin*,
trusted to me! laugh sore tooth
sucked warm, sweet; sweet wine

running cool through new
dry shrewd turnings of my soul,
opening veins.

Gull-feathers beating,
beating! Gliding. Still,
sidelong eye . . . wings beating

like words against my eyes.
And your eyes—
o brother-animal, mild,

terrible!—your eyes wait, have been waiting,
knowing,
unknowable, on that sky shore.

A life is waiting.
Its webbed hand
reached out. . .

Trust me!
truth-
telling fish of the sky!

your hand beyond my hand,
your phosphorous trail
broken, lost.

Visiting Day at School

'She knows she can rub some of her
brown skin off and use it for coloring.'
—A mother, to Robert Coles

The tall, good, raw-boned, wrong
teacher teaches wrong
glory the children shuffle back from dumb

as we do, too,
having got the problem
right:

what you hold
in your hand
is your hand:

You shall all have prizes, and the last,
they say, first: to come home free,
warm and bare, to laugh to see, Jack,

see the years run
around the tree
to melt to feed you,

Jane, see the line the days flew,
quick bird, down around the thumb,
almost straight,

through all the king's gold,
back.

The Child Jung

'What will become of the boy?'
—his father

"This stone is,
was for ages,
and will be: knows I know,

and it's good, hidden,
hidden I'm a great old doctor, whirling,

an eighteenth-century man whirling
through the woods in a light green carriage,

buckles on my shoes . . . Schoolboy!
the filthiest boy ever made,

or blessed . . . oh curled black
shivering freak!
O my stone God quicksand Eternity!"

Coltrane, Syeeda's Song Flute

'When I came across it on the piano it reminded
me of her, because it sounded like a happy,
child's song.'
—Coltrane

To Marilyn, to Peter,
playing, making things: the walls, the stairs,
the attics, bright nests in nests;
the slow, light, grave unstitching of lies,
opening, stinking, letting in air

Pilgrims (1969) | 91

you bear yourselves in, become your own mother and father,
your own child.
You lying closer.

You going along. Days.
The strobe-lit wheel stops dead
once, twice in a life: old-fashioned rays:

and then all the rest of the time pulls blur,
only you remember it more, playing.

Listening here in the late quiet you can think
great things of us all, I think we will all, Coltrane,
meet speechless and easy in Heaven, our names
known and forgotten, all dearest, all come giant-stepping
out into some wide, light, merciful mind . . .

John
Coltrane, 40, gone
right through the floorboards,
up to the shins, up to the eyes,
closed over,

Syeeda's happy, child's song
left up here, playing.

Photograph of Delmore Schwartz

A young king,
oak, painted and gilded, writing

no one should be so unhappy,
holding his hands out,

but his arms are missing from the shoulders down,
his right side's gone, his mouth's

flaking like a mirror, still
photograph of your childhood,

your son. No one
should be so unhappy, should lie

still in that bending room
where all the atoms fly

off their hooks, animals and children
and friends kill, it was a delusion,

we were not living, the hotel floor
wasn't coming and going and coming

at that great head hurled radiant, flat
at the new world.

The Torn-down Building

Slowly, slowly our exploding time
gives off its lives: a lens, an eyelash rub
under the new ground broken,
under the new primary-colored paint
put up for someone to come to
to start off from to cherish

but dear one this December
the walls walk off, we sit mother-naked
smiling on our boxes of books:
slowly the first snowfall

Pilgrims (1969) | 93

curls around its own faint fall
each dot different we thought we could
turn back and back to learn, with all this
light everywhere.

The snow falls around as we walk talking war,
books, the times, our friends' funny business.
Lens, eyelash whisper against the flat
stairs outlined in old paint on the open air:
the light draws a thousand thousand window sills,
bottles, our shadows on the floor,
all backs, our piles of books, our toys,
our boxes of letters. Slowly over the newspaper
this quarter century takes in
its infant deaths, gives off its smiling *kouroi*
and we will meet their eyes in the air

    The January light's stock still
a second from your face to mine, mine to the child's,
her words a flare, a fountain lighter than air.

Moon Man
    for A.R

        'Here too we dare to hope.'
        —Romano Guardini

Swimming down to us
light years
not always a straight line
that was his joke, his night
fears, his pilgrim's climb.

About half way
throwing his silver
suit away he
sees the green earth
click for the first time:

the lightest girl
the heaviest ocean
coming to themselves
and to his hand.

He sets a comradely couple walking
down his white road,
hospitable; hears a shiny
boy and girl, bird and bird
having a time

in his green water.
Clean against it all
one last hour
all alone the moon man's
open everywhere:

This mass is his salt
his girl
       his sky
his work
       his floor.

The Child and the Terrorist, The Terrorist and the Child

The globe's on fire in his hands
and everyone's asleep.

Pilgrims (1969) | 95

What will we feed him when he comes?
Just getting to know his step, his voice,

my step, a way back in the dark
to where I go without telling lies

or leaving anyone, will take a lifetime,
and it's going slowly,

                        and there's that blue-
white shell I turned my back on at my back,

cracked, stuck to me bone by bone,
turning to stone, wanting to drop,
wanting to turn in a cool globe,
wanting to call

—You, how is it with you?
Archaically cut off. Antarctic miles.

Night

From this night on God let me eat
like that blind child on the train
touching her yogurt as I'd touch a spiderweb
the first morning in the country—sky red—

holding the carton and spoon to her mouth
with all her eyeless body, and then
orientally resting, the whole time smiling
a little to one side of straight ahead.

Pilgrims

Standing there they began to grow skins
dappled as trees, alone in the flare

of their own selves: the fire
died down in the open ground

and they made a place for themselves.
It wasn't much good—
they'd fall, and freeze,

some of them said
Well, it was all they could do,

some said it was beautiful, some days,
the way the little ones took to the water,
and some lay smoking, smoking,

and some burned up for good,
and some waited,
lasting, staring
over each other's merciful shoulders,
listening:
      only high in a sudden January thaw
or safe a second in some unsmiling eyes
they'd known always

whispering
Why are we in this life.

Ordinary Things

1974

Chalk lines still mark the floor
just where you stood. Our shoulders touched.
I was afraid. You were just saying
ordinary things.
—Huub Oosterhuis,
"Twenty Days' Journey"

Ordinary Things (1974) | 101

PART I

After Elegies

Almost two years now I've been sleeping,
a hand on a table that was in a kitchen.

Five or six times you have come by
the window; as if I'd been on a bus

sleeping through the Northwest, waking up,
seeing old villages pass in your face,

sleeping.
             A doctor and his wife, a doctor too, are in the kitchen
area, wide awake. We notice things
differently: a child's handprint in a clay plate, a geranium, aluminum
balconies rail to rail, the car horns of a wedding,

blurs of children in white. *LIFE* shots
of other children.   Fire to paper; black

faces, judge faces, Asian faces; flat
earth   your face   fern   coal

'Autumn Day'

> *Who has no house now will not build him one...*
> *Will waken, read, and write long letters...*
> *—Rilke, 'Autumn Day'*

The house in the air is rising, not
settling between any trees.
Its lines may have come here by machine,
wirephoto, they soften to dots in the rain.

What draws you on so hard?
  You would like to think
about resting
a minute on the mobbed walk or
the electrocardiograph table
    to ask about the house there—dark,
    stone, floating out over the edge of the buildings,
    someone, something, it may be, inside—
but you can't stop here: the dangerous air,
the crowds, the lights, the hardening Indian Summer. . .

  strange quiet,
with time for work, your evenings, you will write long letters
this winter, you have your friends,
and the names of friends of friends.

He said,

"When I found where we had crashed, in the snow, the two of us,
alone, I made a plan. It takes all my energy to like it.
The trees keep thinning, and the small animals.
She swims over me every night like warmth, like my whole life
going past my eyes. She is the sleep they talk about, and some days
all I can want is sleep."

Ordinary Things (1974) | 103

Forces

This man, blind and honored,
listens to his student reader;
this man did what he thought
and sickens in jail; another
comes to the end of his work;
another threw himself out.

Us too, our destinies get on,
into middle age.

Today we visited a field of graves—
slaves' or Indians' graves, you said—
sunk, unmarked, green edges of hammered granite
sharp as a shoulder blade.
                                        God break me out
of this stiff life I've made.

Kin

A woman's face at the window,
white, composed, tells me I
do not love her; I did not love him;
I do not love my children, so they wither,
so she will take them, take them away.

I cannot love him: he is dead. And she—
she will not hurt us now.

But the somber child;
and the wind, and the white window.

Anesthesia

Right after her birth they crowded in,
into the white room, huge tall masks
of women's faces
brick-red lips, chalked-in triangular eyes
gazed at us: nothing; said:
nothing; not-women they were suicides, trees, soft,
pale, freckled branches bending over her—
I knew them as my own, their cries
took on the family whiskey voice, refusal,
need,—their human need peeled down, tore,
scratched for her life—
I hacked and hacked them apart—

then who knows
when you murder things like that
who comes in and takes over

After Elegies (2)

The doctors tell me, "Swim.
You are beginning, moving on; yes,
trailing his side, still
amazed at your own body apart; yes, looking back,
you don't have to smile that way, afraid
we are not here; you are beginning,
leaving nothing; your friend is here
with you, and you know him,
and all your old desire;
but in a queer tranquillity.
Yourselves. No reason any more
why not."

Ordinary Things (1974) | 105

PART II

3 A.M. in New York

I have been standing at the edge
of this green field all night.
My hand is sticky with sugar.

The village winks; it thinks it is
the muscle of the world. The heart.
The mouth.

The horse is standing across the field, near the fence.
He doesn't come any closer,
even in the dark, or run away.

Blood memory:
fixed on vacancy:
coming back and back for a sign

the fat of his coat
the shut out of his eye.

Space

Keeping to my room
the cut in my thumb
took on more interest than the thumb

the dark a clean success
after the changing mask
of his face,

and my body—
its hypnotic
ticking over and over,

wanting, not wanting,
in all that hard-edged, squared-off, positive
concrete, aluminum.

I let it go,
all seven years and seven years.

I'm weightless, free   unwritten space

How do they get from minute to minute here?

Far off, low,
a little stir begins, a word, a missed

beat, a listening: this-
world, this-world.

Letter from a Country Room

Off without you
I hang around in the middle distance, walking, talking,
working   made-up mindwork
to send to the city Michael
where you are, where you write
   "She's coming back from the coast next week,
   I don't know what then"
A moth beats at the screen,
the thin, yellow dotted curtain lifts, tacked to the soft
scribbled-over wood   *signed QB + FB*   *8/15-(69)*
                Nothing   *Fuck War*

To   *No Peace, Jaybo?*

Worry About

The sky streams hollowness, no city cover of light.
I follow, where they go,
someone's house,
I go, dim, incognito: tacked
to the way things are. Everything streams:
dumbstruck, stopped stock-still: you too: Jaybo!
Our quiet
trustful sides
pro
tec
ted
anyhow down the whole 200 miles.

A Child's Death

I remember the dark spaces,
black sand islands rising on the x-rays:
what I couldn't touch.

Not like this world,
our old solid,
where we multiply;

not this blurred body
merely her history.

Revolution

Here is a man.
Behind him
dark, in front of him
dark. The fuse the world lit
races up his spine. Blows up
his son who holds by him,
his love of women,
his learning   his wanting
late now to be touched   to touch.
An ordinary man. Thou
red black white slight scattered

thing o women's animal-song o slant
blown up drift arch dead white
song white powder   women rocking rocking
nowhere to lay your head
fox bird woman and man
O come   and out of nothing   whiteness
they come, tearing their shirts off,
alone, together, touching,
not touching, friends, who are the living
who were the dead?

Three Voices One Night in the Community Kitchen

A MAN:
"Jeb was hitting her in the face, I sat there, not doing anything.
Her face was open, as if he wasn't hurting her. He didn't look angry.
He sat back and they were smiling at each other. He knew her
better than I did. I wanted to kill Jeb, I didn't even get up. I haven't
even said what really happened."

Ordinary Things (1974) | 109

A WOMAN:
"I was sitting in the back seat. Another woman we both knew, but
an old friend of his, was sitting in the front seat beside him. He was
shouting at her. She wanted me to help her, to get out, but then it
changed. She was alone in the car with him. He was driving.
She tried to touch his shoulder, he shrugged her off, he was looking
straight ahead, singing, talking to the drivers of the other cars."

A MAN:
"The books are all wrong. Besides you've never read them.
"You are another person.
"I've told you all about it, maybe you don't remember.
"I had a very long, very sad dream I just wanted to see human face."

The Knife

In my sleep:
Fell at his feet   wanted to eat him right up
would have   but
even better
he talked to me.

Did I ask you to?
Were those words my blood-sucking too?

Now I will have a body again
move differently, easier   back to the plan
a little house   a woman and a man

crossed against yours my soul will show
glow through my breastbone:
Back down into the kitchen
yours

Here   I will save you
others have failed, even died, but I
will save you   you save me   devour me away
up

Woke up:
I can cry but I can't wake up
today again   don't answer the door
then did   couldn't look at you   talk

couldn't place the bed in the room, or where the room was
when I closed my eyes

This is the same old knife   my knife
I know it as well as I know my own mouth
It will be lying there on the desk if

I open my eyes I will know the room very well
there will be the little thrown-out globe of blood we left
and every molecule of every object here will swell
with life. And someone will be at the door.

Seeing *L'Atalante*
(Directed by Jean Vigo, 1934)

A woman sits at her workable, reading stories,
thinking of all the true stories she'd never tell
out of love, and shame, root fear: broken glass, torn walls.
Reading stories about rivers (she is the river),
rafts crossing over, father, husband, lover,
her own sons. The river sings; he has always thought that. Stories.
The stories cross over.

Ordinary Things (1974) | 111

On the raft he makes a shelter
for her, fills a glass (sees her trembling, clear),
tries to sleep.
Hours, hours, is he sleeping or swimming. Save her, save
them, leave them alone, his voice beats, his lungs, his heart,
his arms beat, beat, so slowly,   the wavering dark and the dark is
smiling, wanting their smile, their faces for its own.

PART III

Twenty Days Journey by Huub Oosterhuis
Translated from the Dutch with Judith Herzberg

Twenty Days' Journey

1
I thought   it's only a thin threshold
a step scattered with straw.

It is a vertical stairway
a desert   steep with pyramids.

I edge down slopes. Dead bodies
shrug down past me. All their books.
Sentenced world, poisoned dream,
you are the most alone, the meanest.

The key I hold on to melts in my hand
I dig a pit
walk on   turn back
not a track anywhere

I bend to the wind
stalk this earth
hate my feet.

112 | *Light Me Down: The New & Collected Poems of Jean Valentine*

2

Wearing a veined marble vest
I sit at the game table, play,
play for life or death

for the blown-away footstep
in the snow
the voice that called me.

3

Who stumbles across the broken
field grass (foreground, left) and onto
the wide rusted wheel   falls   and then spins
and then stops   tries to think   runs on
across an island   am I.

The one who lies across the huge gold dome
(top center)   who lies   lips stretched to bursting
is you. Someone is still between us   almost
flesh   almost visible
tipped at the bottom of a blue-
brown river   like an old bottle.

4

Flood me then
stone that rushes red through the dam
fear tomorrow this moment
dry wood of imagining
dim awareness of *then*   now torn open
skinned alive.
My mind is lead, every cell
hard, heavy, metallic.

I climb up onto a road   trip
over the edge, fall
into your glass depth
you   beaker filled with fire

Ordinary Things (1974) | 113

my body turns to mist but still stays alive,
an eye that will not close

5
20 days' journey: I pack vapor   fold air
make etchings of water on water
—see you standing there
but without a face   diamond death.

6
You are splintered into me
bits of soft denture
biting into my lips
useless pain   I am nothing   a brain pan
a cup holding your voice.
The chipped scales of your skin
crust my eyes closed
your palate slowly grows
into my mouth
your face grows out of my pores
like a feverish rash.
As if I never was
you cut your way out through every part of me
I become flesh of your flesh
bone of your bone.

7
Chalk lines still mark the floor
just where you stood. Our shoulders touched.
I was afraid. You were just saying
ordinary things.

Much became little   the mail
was left lying for days.
Nowhere now—
my sense of you everywhere

8
When they fired from the sea
onto a town
then   where the dead
stood on end like ropes
then   with the firing on Khe Sanh
it was then.

When a thin sac drifted down
out of the sky   hurled pillars
hands spattered   you called me

You had been living there a long time
you were taken
eyelids lips fingers and all
thrown against me
you   a bridge   a path through death.

I stood out in the sea, up to my waist in water
and took pictures of the fragments
the playing field   like a man's back.
The skipping survivors.

9
In small patches
it has clotted
become glass

something like a house
but empty

a shape
under a bright silk scarf.

I rub sand
into my eyes
so I won't see anything.

I hear you walk
as if you were carrying something:

your feet
grown back.

10
We walked
along the sea
the coastline broke like a thread.

I rang for days at the door
a long talk going on and on
through me like a wire

I crawled to the roof
where you were
when I got there you were gone.

PART IV

This Hate

It is like a fitting room only
with eight or nine
mirrors instead of three—

only, no door.
But you see: no ceiling. They never do.
I love them, my mother, my daughter. Both. I do, and I can write it
out and seal it

but it hurts, the mirrors closing in.
Now: the stamp.
I have to do this very carefully,

looking up; I feel, you see, the fontanel's   gentle
beat   at closing.

Carefully now—the shine is blinding—
I have to jump and drop it out, over.

Now I need a skin.
Or maybe this fogging up
transparency is It. Is it?
It feels like yours, more or less;
only for the face.

This Minute

The videotape runs
silent, but life-size.
A bed. A woman
and a man. A woman
and a man.
A woman and a woman.
An old man and a child.
A boy and a middle-aged woman.
Two women and a man
upside-down one
woman and two men

—The long black torn shades in the classroom
flicker like pigeons. The A/V man or his boy
shuts the windows.
—Coney Island   blurred
density   a still.

A bed again, a man
alone holding himself

Ordinary Things (1974) | 117

there. Now a woman
sitting on the bed alone

writing on a filmstrip,
I'll ask when it's over
I think but
it starts over

with this time
—did they last time?—real
faces and breasts and
hands and crotches and

I stay to see it again
to see if it's me writing
it, that woman at the end,
that might make it easier or

not. Or I might be
one of the others.
Or not.—A siren goes by
down on the street, stiffening our spines.—No I'm not her
or anyone in it at all but here
it starts over and this time
—were they last time?—
all my friends.

You're in it this time,
and me, too,
but each off   alone   clear
in the shot that was a still,

Coney Island, but animated
now, walking
smoking
playing the transistor radio.

Watching, you
touch my hand
with the hand not holding the radio and say
you never loved me so much

as this minute. The A/ V man
switches on the light, says "Quiet!" and I see
all our friends are here
watching. And here it starts over.

Couvre-Feu: after Paul Eluard
   (in peacetime)

What could you expect
we were in a strange city, we saw no one,
we had almost no money, it was cold,
we went by different names, we hoped to see no one,
we went out mostly at night, it was cold,
what could you expect
on the streets they were all going home, carrying flowers,
every paper said you are doing these things
for the last time, every silence said
this has nowhere to go,

The green walls held.
We know what we knew
what could you expect
the narrow city
shone in all night on our room
what could you expect
we were one flesh one bone.

Ordinary Things (1974) | 119

Fidelities

1
Up in this quiet room here, reading your letter,
it's as if I'm in your house. I'm reading.
You're working late, downstairs. The children are all asleep.
It's raining. Later we'll have some warm bourbon and water,
and sleep.
     Outside, the streets are white, the rain
shines like glass. Police
cruise by. You hold me in your arms.
Huge planes move off overhead.

It's as if
if I answer your letter I'll have to show them
my passport: New York. October.
Other friends, another life. It's as if I could choose.

2
strange, sad, these letters

not knowing what you're thinking, reading this
Friendships, fidelities.
Things as they are.
     Out in the Sheep Meadow
I stare at the high school lovers lying, hardly moving, their skin
shining under the gray trees; I stare
at the old people, talking together, their faces
up to the sun. As if they were talking in bed.

My hand lying open in your hand. . .

The Sunday papers the dreamy bicycle-riders

        As things are
I hate, I want to embrace the man, the woman who is near you,
who hears your step.

120 | *Light Me Down: The New & Collected Poems of Jean Valentine*

3
not even knowing where you are

Your quick, hunched-forward walk
in this man's walk, your eyes
in that old woman's gray, restless eyes.

4
We have our lives.

The river shone white-yellow under the yellow sky; every insect shone,
rising and dropping. We walked back up the field to the house.

Your room there. This white room. Books, papers, letters.
Stamps, the telephone. Our lives.
Were always choosing our lives.

5
All night I thought I heard the phone, or a child
crying. Your face
turned into a snapshot of your face, one
from five years ago.

Your wife and I were sitting up late
in the kitchen, drinking coffee, talking like sisters.
A child cried; one of us went to her, held her.

Here, sitting up late, with a friend,
listening, talking, touching her hand, his hand,
I touch your hand. No one
says anything much. No one leaves anyone.

Ordinary Things (1974) | 121

Susan's Photograph

I am the razor that has been put away, also
the wrist in the photograph,
and—lately—also the photographer,
the friend, the taxi, the hospital room,
the three other women, their visitors, the flowers,
and the nurse.

At the end of that summer
I started going to paramedical school
at night. Days I still talk to my students
about all the dead
overexcitable poets; all their friends;
and the living; and show the old newsreels
where they keep leaving each other, old
people, children, soldiers; and the parades:
the general, the waving people, the black horses, the black
limousines, the mules, the tall gray puppets.

But this photograph here:
a Woman in a country room, in western Massachusetts,
in peace, so sad and grained:
        now I see you look up, outside the frame—
this room here, friends, a table, a book or two,
paper, see you have all you need,
—even in prison you would have your childhood—
see you go on and do what you ought to do,

it is enough, now,
anywhere, with
everyone you love there to talk to.

Outside the Frame

It is enough, now, anywhere,
with everyone you love there to talk to.

And to listen.
Slowly we can tell each other some things about our lives:
runs, rests, brief resolutions; falls, and lulls;
hard joyful runs, in certainty; dull, sweet
durances, human silences;
                              look back in at the children,
the regular, neutral flicker of their blood; pale, solemn,
long-legged animal-gods in their sleep,
growing into their lives, in their sleep.

Forces (2): Song

Weeds breaking up through stone:
our hold on our own hollows, the quick,
curved line of a smile: bare, our own
ribs shelter us: a boy's cold, white
fingers around a match:
heart belling. hollow, quick,
through the live horn, the bone, to this
day, calm.

The Messenger

1979

for James Shea

My name comes to me like an angel.
—Tomas Tranströmer

THE MESSENGER

Beka, 14

Squat, slant-eyed, speaking in phrase-book phrases, the messenger
says he is your brother, and settles down on his heels
to wait, muffled in flat, supple skin, rope over his shoulder. You
wait, play, turn, forget. Years,

years. The messenger is both like the penguin
who sits on the nest of pebbles, and the one
who brings home pebbles to the nest's edge in his beak,
one at a time, and also like the one
who is lying there, warm, who is going to break out soon:

becoming yourself: the messenger is growing
strong, tough feet for land,
and strong wings for the water, and long
butter-yellow feather eyebrows, for looks. And will speak,
calmly, words you already know: "thread," "island,"

"must": now, slowly, just while you lie on your cot there, half-
dozing, not reading, watching the trees,
a summer, and a summer; writing long pages, tearing them up;

lying there under the close August window, while at your back
the water-lit, dotted lines of home start coloring in.

Dufy Postcard

The postcard taped on your white kitchen wall has roses, in a white
bowl, on the blue and green shadowed table; the table is brown,
yellow. Down the wallpaper's field of pink roses, a violet shadow

turns brown, moves across the floor: now the lines go off the card,
the lines of the walls, one curved foot of the round table, the
oblong shadow; the floor ends mid-air, here:

You sitting at your table
looking at the postcard. Green
day lights the windows; everyone
still asleep. Taut lines.

Day, with its hours, and buildings;
people start, around you. You wait
a minute more in the white room—
white tent against the snowed-over path, the wind,
familiar voice—*one life*—

Every day you move farther outside
the outlines, kinder, more dangerous.
Where will you be going.
Who will the others be.

The Field

> *"There is a strange power in bog water which prevents decay. Bodies
> have been found which must have lain in bogs for more than
> a thousand years . . ."* —*A Danish Almanack of 1837.*
> —P.V. Glob, *The Bog People*

A sculpture in a bare white gallery:
Pike jaws arch, in a shining transparent space
without locality: levels of peat, sand, air.
Bones. Teeth.
Fine, thin white jaws: the willingness to do harm—Odysseus
         leaving—

At forty we have always been parents; we hold each other's sex
in a new tenderness . . . As we were; hardly breathing
over the pulse in the infant's lucent temple—

The Messenger (1979) | 127

Our breath comes shorter,
our lives have been a minute, a feather, our sex is chaff . . .

Sleep: the room
breaks up into blue and red
film, long muscles crossing bones, raw pelvis pulled
to birth: Incised on stone, bronze, silver
Eyes, belly, mouth   Circle on circle—

Look, by morning noises, in this city island flickering with gold
          flame,
These photographs.
The Tollund man. The Windeby girl. The goddess
Nerthus.

In the middle of a light wood of tall forked trees stripped white
at the edge of a bog, in Denmark,
we walk   slowly out to the field   walk slowly by
the hacked-out cots
of silk
bog children.

Living Together

Dawn, streaks of rose-brown, dry—
A car starts up. A needle veers,
an hour, a summer . . . Day
settles back, on the last
century, our trying, our Biblical
conviviality.

This should, should not, happen, these
two people met, or not then, not now;
or now.

Out in the white Judaic light
you move like figures in a lesson;

You open your life like a book.
Still I hear your story
like a parable, where every word is simple,
but how does this one
go with the one before, the next . . .

Here Now

The sky is the same changing
colors as the farthest snow.
The tall pines float
like candles with the current,
next to the stream
clear with brown leaves.

>   A pitched ceiling,
>   two cots; apple petals;
>   the thin smell of woodsmoke,
>   wood, turpentine . . .
>   *My sister, I*, who
>   we were then—

>   Downstairs, the grown world
>   bent to its books; low flames, low
>   voices. Sleeplessness . . .

>   Our wooden room
>   —The white cloth
>   on the table between us

The Messenger (1979) | **129**

Forty years, a breath . . . our tall daughters circle like birds, in our
light houses, bump into things
Their high words, leaving out their lives

Quiet-minded, a lightness, this morning; the piece of sea glass next
to the window, almost amber, curved like a thumb, a petal

The sky is the same changing
blue, and green, as the burning snow.
So much must be asleep
under this white quiet, sleep,
sleep, low voices, dust hair,
under the eyes
the impossible
compass fingers
of the god.

The Forgiveness Dream: Man from the Warsaw Ghetto

He looked about six or seven, only much too thin.
It seemed right he would be there, but everything,
every lineation, was slow . . . He was speaking in Polish,
I couldn't answer him.
He pointed at the window, the trees, or the snow,
or our silver auditorium.

I said to him in English, "I've lived the whole time
here, in peace. A private life."   "In shame,"
I said. He nodded. He was old now, kind,
my age, or my mother's age: He nodded,
and wrote in my notebook—"Let it be good."

He frowned, and stopped,
as if he'd forgotten something,

and wrote again,
"Let it."

I walk, and stop, and walk—
touch the birch bark   shining, powdery, cold:
taste the snow, hot on my tongue—
pure cold, licked from the salt of my hand:

This quiet, these unvisitable stars
move with choices.
Our kin are here.
Were here.

Turn

This is the new apartment   new
painted livingroom
its table, its bed, its chair.
It is floating, and the earth's bright rim
is floating through an indifferent blank, without
color, without consolation—

> The pregnant woman with a child at home
> rests, has a cup of tea, closes her eyes . . .
> I want to walk in the winter field again . . .
> Was peacefulness
> ever what we were after?
> She thinks of the child, who wants the tea, who wants
> her eyes, her mouth, her hands,
> who pulls her out to the field
> to the thick of things
> away from the thick of things.

A woman stands   at the new window.
Torso: a bronze Matisse back:

in the Museum garden. Its children playing, still,
inside its hollow part.
Its strength thickens, simplifies.
Grows quieter.

The first day's quiet. The second; the second
year. I'm taking up my life. If you were here
who am I honest with
I'd have to think a long time
to say the simplest thing:
nothing like anything I know.

Prayer in Fever

The hospital shuts down to its half-night.

I stand back,
talk in words from some book:
The wall could be the floor.
Everything you look at
is changed by your looking at it

This packed dirt square, these wires . . . somewhere someone must
run for it, black hair, red mouth, burn
strips of fish on a green edge of the Hudson,
under a cloud of stars, under bridge lights, they must hunch down,
talk to each other, touch each other, the way this thin bright snow
masses, this blind oval pulling

gold   across the ceiling
floating out
off the fold-
back of space

The day does rise. The turning gaze of the river:
So many eyes. So calm.

The gray green curve of earth still
waiting   with us
holding us
huge curved mosaic hands

your hand
—how would you bide so long?

Working

in memory of Robert Lowell
1917-1977

Under the high rooms,
under the trains, the talk,
you kept digging down

from life to life
to come across earth's fragments:
the child; the century's children;

the ones we do not know yet,
because they were flesh—

their secret, lilted home-
voices, faces caught
in lightning.   Found there

earth's bone-shadowed eyes;
her still life
your awkward printing:

starvation: light
moving down and up through light . . .

A ladder of stuff: a soft, gray,
broken oar, a feather,
a shoe, a child's pencil case;

light drawing us
to light,
day speaking to day . . .

Now, at dusk,
the man digging
saw himself approaching:

his half-smile looked past us: past himself:

the man chipping, at dusk,
under the trains, digging up,
the dark, prosperous bluestone.

Silences: A Dream of Governments

From your eyes I thought
we could almost move   almost speak
But the way your face
held there, in the yellow air,
And that hand, writing down our names—
And the way the sun
shone right through us
Done with us

        Then
the plain astonishment—the air

broken open: just ourselves
sitting, talking; like always;
the kitchen window
propped open by the same
blue-gray dictionary.
August. Rain. A Tuesday.

Then, absence. The open room
suspended   The long street
gone off   quiet, dark.
The ocean floor. Slow
shapes glide by

Then, day
keeps beginning again: the same
stubborn pulse against the throat,
the same
listening for a human voice—
your name, my name

After Elegies (3)

Here in the close, most clear sun,
on this worn wood porch, halfway
over the beating harbor,
under the round sky—the daylight moon's
luminous, fragile skull—

Halfway between sleep and waking,
I think of you,
my older brother,
difficult friend; and your moving on
from us to the dead
seems a few blocks' walk;
seems nothing.

Are you nothing   Nowhere we can find you

—But you look up
from your spread-out books and papers, you say
—But now I can't hear what you're saying,
and how can you hear us now?

or see our rowing progress here? our bare arms
pulled—
          Earth pulled
to where it would not go.

The Messenger

I / The Father

In the strange house
in the strange town
going barefoot past the parents' empty room
I hear the horses   the fire   the wheel   bone wings
your voice.

I make my corners:
this table
this letter
this walk.

The night you died
by the time I got there to the Peter Bent Brigham Hospital
the guard said, It's no use your going up.
That was the first time you spoke to me dead—
from the high corner of the lobby.

136 | *Light Me Down: The New & Collected Poems of Jean Valentine*

The next night a friend said, Well these deaths
bring our own deaths, close.

But now, this is your voice
younger than mine; leaning over—say goodbye—
the fake gold Navy officer's sword
the square real gun.

Every night the freight train crossed the grown-over road
at the foot of the Neilsens' field, trailing its rusty
whistle. The fire, the wheel; fireflies.
The wall of stars. Real horses. I could go
anywhere. I could go to where you are.
I lie under the bank, my face on the wall of wet grass.
I can't go anywhere, No such thing my dear.

My mother has flour on her hands,
on her cheekbone. My father smiles his one smile
gray and white on the wall. She pushes
her hair back from her eyes. His eyes
settle. On us.

II / The Messenger

You are the messenger
my half-brother, I have seen you before,
you have visited me before,
in the hallways of a school, a hospital,
in the narrow hotel room once,
once on a dirt road in August.

I lean on the oak grain of this desk,
the grain of your body, your hair,
your long back. This plum
is darker than your mouth
I drink its salty sweetness   its leaf-smell
from your tongue. Sleep;

The Messenger (1979) | 137

your dark head at my breasts

                             turns
to a boy's head, you are Allan   my brother
Johnny DeSoto, nine
Philip   my brother
David

Your hand is my father's sure, square hand,
it is not too late, digging down through the sand
to show me the water

You turn, say something in your sleep

You are my sister   I hold you warm in my hand   her breast
You trace my breasts

My eyes were clenched, they are opening . . .
everything, nothing . . .
We aren't afraid.
The earth drips through us

Now I want to live forever
Now I could scatter my body easily
if it was any use

now that the earth
has rained through us
green   white
green green grass.

You say you came to say if I live without you
I'll live. That's always been your story.

III / The Hill

The dogwood blossoms stand in still, horizontal planes
at the window. In mist. Small gray figures

climb away up the green hill. Carrying precision tools wrapped in
    oilcloth
Some push their bicycles. —Wait, I'm coming, no this time I mean
    it

now I could scatter my body
if it was any use

saying again
if you do not teach me I shall not learn

—First, you see, you must be still. Touch nothing.
Here, in this room. To look at nothing, to listen to nothing.
A long time. First, you see, you must open your clenched hands.
You must carry your mother and your father at your breasts.

I stand on all fours, my fur
is warm; warm organs, the male and the female.
The earth is light and warm around us.
We lick our cracked old worries
like blood away from our faces, our haunches, we
nudge each other, all our white fur, goodbye, goodbye . . .

saying again there is a last
even of last times

I wake up with one hand holding hard to the other hand.
My head rests on oilcloth. A quiet voice laughs, and says again,

—You were going to go without me?
That was always your story.

TWO TRANSLATIONS

Huub Oosterhuis: Orpheus

Orpheus like a farmer
behind his plow of flutes
found in a dream the wound   the damp
place where the earth
quivers like a windpipe
and went down there.

Having been driven through woods
turned to rock   shifted by ice
fingers worn out with sailing
he got past the dog
and saw they were all dead there
except Eurydice.

Who lived in a barrel of zinc
brightly lit up
and had her love's doorframe
staves of a bed   a tree
swelling about her own underleaf white
sloping body
waiting for him but almost
unknowingly.

Enlisted with god he served seven years
shepherd   doorman   or he threaded wires
that would blow up thresholds   sink boats
direct the sun
and, to claim her, he became
wisely poorer.

Sometimes thought I'll walk into the countryside
like a horse

won't eat   will drown
it's better so
But did not want to and knew why not
the next day and the following he did his work
and waited.

After another seven years she could come along
it was as if he felt the worn spots
all over her
she had grown aimless
fat from sitting and sleeping
Could it be the snake   the thirst
he thought, when I play the flute
she may follow   she may
once again turn beautiful
as she used to be.

All right then she follows him
and why shouldn't she
she is nobody else and his tall back
is older is more hairy
but still the one she always
used to caress.

Then suddenly he no longer knew
whether it was she
the tune having escaped him
The forest as in every underworld
was doing well he saw
what had decayed was resurrected
He did not look back.

Sleeping they go on without a sound
She dreams   You and I were walking
I'm waking up
the skins over my eyes are still black
from waiting for your eyes   Look at me

The Messenger (1979) | **141**

if you love me she calls
Run still faster

Running on stripped nerves   I have
not looked around he calls and we shall
dearest see the earth
until our second death.
Over the water
sunlight blows before the wind
the grass is dark   creatures pass by
He walks and no longer knows
whether or not he did look back
and where the earth is
underneath   above

Osip Mandelstam: 394

Toward the empty earth
falling, one step faltering—
some sweetness, in this
unwilling hesitance—

she walks, keeping
just ahead of her friends,
the quick-footed girl,
the boy, one year younger.

A shy freedom draws her, her hobbled step
frees her, fires her, and it seems
the shining riddle in her walk
wants to hold her back:

the riddle, that this spring weather
is for us the first mother:

the mother of the grave.
And this will keep on beginning forever.

There are women,
the damp earth's flesh and blood:
every step they take, a cry,
a deep steel drum.

It is their calling
to accompany those who have died;
and to be there, the first
to greet the resurrected.

To ask for their tenderness
would be a trespass against them;
but to go off, away from them—
no one has the strength.

Today an angel; tomorrow
worms, and the grave;
and the days after
only lines in chalk.

The step you took
no longer there to take.

Flowers are deathless. Heaven is round.
And everything to be is only talk.

—Voronezh. 4 May 1937

SOLITUDES

*Some of the signs suggest that you feel a leaf or
other part of a plant. A string leads from the top
of the sign to the plant.*
—Braille sign on the Miwok Trail, Muir Woods

The bird a nest, the spider a web, man friendship.
—Blake

December 21st

How will I think of you
"God-with-us"
a name: a word

and trees path stars this earth
how will I think of them

and the dead I love   and all absent friends
here-with-me

and table: hand: white coffee mug:
a northern still life:

and you
without a body

quietness

and the infant's red-brown mouth   a star
at the star of a girl's nipple . . .

144 | *Light Me Down: The New & Collected Poems of Jean Valentine*

Sanctuary

People pray to each other. The way I say "you" to someone else,
respectfully, intimately, desperately. The way someone says
"you" to me, hopefully, expectantly, intensely . . .
—Huub Oosterhuis

You   who I don't know   I don't know how to talk to you

—What is it like for you there?

Here . . . well, wanting solitude; and talk; friendship—
The uses of solitude. To imagine; to hear.
Learning braille. To imagine other solitudes.
But they will not be mine;
to wait, in the quiet; not to scatter the voices—

What are you afraid of?

What will happen. All this leaving. And meetings, yes. But death.
What happens when you die?

". . . not scatter the voices,"

Drown out. Not make a house, out of my own words. To be quiet in
another throat; other eyes; listen for what it is like there. What
word. What silence. Allowing. Uncertain: to drift, in the
restlessness . . . Repose. To run like water—

What is it like there, right now?

Listen: the crowding of the street; the room. Everyone hunches in
against the crowding; holding their breath: against dread.

What do you dread?

What happens when you die?

The Messenger (1979) | 145

What do you dread, in this room now?

Not listening. Now. Not watching. Safe inside my own skin.
To die, not having listened. Not having asked . . . To have scattered
life.

Yes I know: the thread you have to keep finding, over again, to
follow it back to life; I know. Impossible, sometimes.

What Happened

I don't know what happened, some very low time for my friend;
she said, —Come over; she couldn't talk, but come over anyhow.

My friend, have I ever befriended you? Helper and friend, will you
be befriended?

You talked along, quickly, forceably, about this thing and that, as
you do; you handed me coffee; I felt as if we were traveling at
some speed; in a taxi; I was looking at you through glass, you
looked back at me now and then, for a minute, through the glass;
so much grief in your eyes. Almost disinterested—

I asked, —What happened? Then, in your rush of talk, you told
me stories, about old friends, people you met, you showed me books,
photographs I'd like, you fed me, you entertained me.

Am I the unknowable one? Does my listening make just a white
place, like the space a person who is growing blind sees growing on
the page?

Suddenly you stopped walking around the room, stopped smiling.
You sat down, across from me; you said,
        —You and I are the same, in terrible ways.

Then furiously, talking very fast, you told me about my life:
How I go on repeating, over and over, my stupid leap for
home, where there's nothing; a homeless world; what else
did I think I was doing with X, last year; what good did
I think work could do; or anything else; knowing now how
things are: what would I do?

Telling me about your life:
It's always like that: you leap, you think for a minute you
have found something; Nothing; Terrible; there are only
distractions, crowding around over the surface of things.
—Now what would I do. People don't kill themselves, just
because they know how things are, know the world is
like this; they aren't so rational.
Asking yourself:
—What would you do—

To wait. To imagine . . . I just sat there, blind; not-there;
my friend, and I, not seeing each other; seeing instead some mask
or sign; consenting to be some mask or sign.
The half-cured man in Mark's gospel, who answers Christ, "I can
see men as if they were trees, but walking."
To not see, not be seen: the sudden fear: like a déjà vu: is there
anyone I do see? anyone I know? even of the closest ones. Or who
knows me?

To listen for what it is like there. To wait . . . Contagion: our grief
and fury ran down like electricity into the ground, leaving the
room a fiction, an empty space. The glass didn't shift, we
couldn't touch only ghosts: the unreachable teller, the unreachable
listener; both going silent, unbefriended.

—But there are shelters; they break down, but they mend; we
can live, that way. But I didn't say anything; you were telling me
another story, smiling your strong smile, showing me more
things: I couldn't get past them; there wasn't time.

The Messenger (1979) | **147**

I keep talking to you, here, in my head; but I don't know what to
say: not enough:

Yet the cell is only the rudiment. A human being is made up of
about 1,000 billion cells, a drop of blood containing 5 million
of them . . .

To wait. To imagine. Learning braille.

Once I was talking to a friend, a religious man, about the closeness
of friendships in childhood, and he said, What you're talking
about, is God. Mercy on our gropings, our silences. Our harm.
Mercy, or nothing is enough; mercy on our deceptions, endless, our
endless longings; our words that go like smoke into smoke. Some
shelter,
for my friend,
for each one, quiet, talking,
alone, together, to trust, to rest in a while.

Turn (2): After Years

January. At the window
wet-dark twigs and branches of young birch
reach up, cross each other:
a road map, a map of rivers . . .

Hundreds of drops of the freezing rain
hold the day's gray light close:
silver   hundreds of stars

I think of you
looking out your city window—everyone away
—a thin, light-eyed, noticing child,
standing so quiet

—a tall man, restless, faithful, your light eyes always
not-here; always here . . .

I think of our lives
different   the same

the years, half-blown,
        What we had, we have.

Now I can turn,
—now, without want, or harm—
turn back to the room, say your name:
say: *other*   say, *thou* . . .

The Burden of Memory

New Hampshire
January 28th

Do you remember, last time we saw each other, how the first thing
you said was, "Isn't it good we're always friends?" And then, both
of us, I think, feeling stopped, empty-handed; past the high,
brittle day of meeting like lovers, five years ago; just ourselves
again, groping for friendship again. And then, you talked so
easily, like when we were kids; more than you ever have, to me,
about your life, now; yourself.

And I remembered, what I'd known before—I wonder if it's so, for
you, too—being drawn, with you, by memory, back to a life that
seems less harmful . . . "student days" . . . —And what good was
that? That memory itself drawing us to harm.   But then,
ourselves again; some mercy; taking in that angry sorrow, part of
us, a healed bone that does go on hurting; a mark of mercy; and
we could be quiet again, and talk.

The Messenger (1979) | **149**

And then, here in this solitude, this quiet, remembering so many
things I'd forgotten, I was thinking back to those days: you, an
"older man," going with L.; I suppose you were both seventeen . . .
Do you remember, one day when we were talking, I forget what
about, but my saying, "You're such a friend to me," and you said,
"Yes and I always will be." And then I could tell you about that
time, in California. —I want to talk to you now about it, again;
I've never talked to anyone else about it, and it's been alive with
me here again—do you remember it? I don't think you could;
the whole family, over at another Navy family's place, for a picnic.
1943—I was nine. I was off from the other kids when I saw it. In
a shed, or garage, I don't remember: a wooden building, pretty far
off from the house. There was a barrel, but I could see into it, and
there were heads in there, people's heads, cut in half. In something
like formaldehyde maybe, they were kept so life-like. I never knew
why I didn't run for one of the other kids, to look. —I could only
finally tell, on the way home; I got sick again, in the car, and I
told them. Of course my parents said Nonsense, it was impossible;
but very angry. A little later they said I must be very overtired,
and after that they were always very careful that I should get
plenty of sleep. —I could never tell anyone again. It was so real:
but it was impossible, it couldn't have been there. I must be
crazy. And what a creepy kind of crazy. What becomes of people
like that? —And some awful shame, worse than any shame I've
ever felt.

And then I could tell you, that day, ask you, if you thought I was
crazy; tell you about the shame. And you said, "I think it happened.
In some way. I don't know. It doesn't matter, what way."

—You mean a dream or something. I *know* it wasn't a dream. But
I know, it couldn't—

—We were around the same age. I saw things . . . we heard about things.

—But you were there, in the war.

—It doesn't matter. I don't know. It was 1943. People knew things.
We do; we know things now. And here we are, alive. Fine; playing,
in peace. No wonder for the shame. What will we do? I don't
know . . . But it doesn't mean we did those things. *You* know that.

I wonder if you had any idea, how saving that was, what you said.

The same lightening of things, talking to you now, in this room—

And you—I wonder, have I been companionable to you, too,
been there, any use, in your silences, your aloneness—your letter
the other day, saying, "a low time"—I wish I could touch your
hand, there, now . . .

—*We do know things*. That memory, back with me now, and the
shame. Now. *What will we do*

How long can we stay interested in the lone man's liberty? . . .
I'm afraid [the individual], being saved by himself, will be lost
by himself . . . —Montale

February 9th

The consolation of another solitude, miles away, years away; in
the next room; its words, its silences;
waiting to be listened for; imagined.
Kinship.   Meetings.

We all line up to ask each other for help.
Millions.

One.

> *Line up*—in Swedish—associations of people lining up for food,
> shelter . . . — Tranströmer

My whole life, I've never been hungry. Or without a room; with
warmth, and light. Warm; fed. At the edges of this world. People
who *are driven out of their minds by good living.* —Milosz

Aloneness: physical feelings: cold, hunger.   Wrongfulness.
Solitude—choosing to hope to live—holding close in the cold

Emily Dickinson: . . . *test's severe repairs are permitted all.*
                    . . . It is difficult not to be fictitious in so fair a
                    place, but test's severe repairs are permitted all.

Not to be fictitious.
I can't think of the first word.

Uncovering; unthickening. Changes
. . . the memories I can't look out past, to look around: this room—

Look: they join you to every fragility   here

Your letter, from August: *At the same time*
there is such a strong sense, of uncovering
and naming to the point of losing what you
may have had . . . It was like touching the
center and therefore losing it, emptying it
of what you might have been able to hold on to.

> And your letter, saying, *No one has*
> *ever asked me about "everyday life" . . .*
> Raising your son, teaching, in Maine,
> alone painting, paintings not seen
> changing   your memories changing
> *We must account for our existence*
> *and it helps to talk openly if at all*
> *possible. I will try,*

152 | *Light Me Down: The New & Collected Poems of Jean Valentine*

And your letter, saying, *We are*
indeed graced by our mutual friendship
with B_____. She has saved my life more
than once and most especially this fall.
No doubt you have heard from her about

And you, writing, this letter today,
the hidden way of each of us, buried

kinship
a buried crystal holding the sun

kinship
the salt of our hands
touching

changing

memories changing

Higginson: *... I have the greatest desire to see you, always feeling*
that perhaps if I could once take you by the hand I
might be something to you;

Dickinson: *You were not aware that you saved my Life.*

The Messenger (1979) | **153**

"Love and Work":
Freud Dying
—London, September 1939

He could watch his soul, a line drawing, almost a cartoon, rise up,
out of his mouth, past the footpaths up a steep, concentric
mountain, to enter another city: a vast, black and white city,
at the top of space, precisely edged in blue and red and gold leaf.
September. A gray, light absence of God.

All his books were there, in his room; and the rugs over the sofas,
and the small Egyptian statues, the Greek heads. Men and women
with sad, lively eyes came and asked to study with him. Friends
and colleagues were there, "both of the past & of the present."

But the first hour, resting for a minute, from his walk, on a bench
in a green square near his house, he fell asleep. He dreamed he
was walking, deep in the ocean; he was both male and female.
The dome of the world fitted perfectly over the ocean floor. The
slow currents filled his mind with a reasoning peacefulness he
thought he must remember. High clouds of sunlight moved through
the water.

No one here was marked off, by coloring or sex or money. Still, as
they walked slowly by him, their faces held some questioning,
calm sorrow. The dream was like a voice, the singsong rhythms of
a voice he had known a long time, but without words, an old
story. He wondered if someone had told it to him.

He woke up: he wanted to touch someone; to listen, again, to the
consolation of that voice. Familiar voices waited around him in
his room. One spoke his name, a strange sounding word, now.
Most he wanted, to go back to his dream, where there were no Jews,
no saving needed,
and no fame of accomplishment to save them.

No, it must just be that he didn't know anything yet, about that
strange, slow place, its darknesses; he had to go back and listen;
walk there, and think:

Letter from a Stranger

You said, you know what I mean: one winter, you looked and saw
a river branching in the black sycamore branches, silver
veins of roads rising and ending in icy twigs at your window;
an awful time. Then spring came and you said
you *learned to love Lincoln again*; the first leaves came
and you saw Lincoln's *kind, grave face, drawn there*
in the leaves, in the light.
How can I answer your letter? words from your life
bring me home to my life. So safe
now, that I can leave it again, now
the milky quiet. The warm straw.

"Actuarial File"

Orange peels, burned letters, the car lights shining on the grass,
everything goes somewhere—and everything we do—nothing
ever disappears. But changes. The roar of the sun in photographs.
Inching shorelines. Ice lines. The cells of our skin; our meetings,
our solitudes. Our eyes.

A bee careens at the window here; flies out, released: a life
without harm, without shame.   That woman, my friend,
circling against her life, a married life; that man, my friend,
solitary, anarchic, driving away from home; them driving, to each
other—

I know, the hard, half-lost, knowing will; the cold first loneliness
again, outside the commonweal, unmoving;

But to say, *I know*—is there any touch in it?

The words in my dream: "actuarial file." *Actuary, 1. A
registrar or notary, who keeps records of the acts of a court* . . .

To be there; to listen; not invade. Another solitude . . .

I watch her face. The lines of will, kindness, hunger. Silence. She
moves from one thing to another thing in the kitchen, looks out
the window at the other apartment windows . . . A woman moves
around, across the courtyard, making supper. How many people is
she making supper for? Now the woman waters the plants. What
is she thinking about. Her head, her arm, look peaceful . . .

"Everything that happens, happens once and for all. Is this true?
If so, what then?"

Yes. Your story; all of your hope; what you do, breaks. Changes.
"If so, what then?" Nothing disappears. And you do last;

The words in the open page of her notebook, *I'm so cold. My
head hurts.*

Come stay here, at my place, a while. —Someday we will be able
to say, I did this thing; I did that other thing; I was that woman.
Someday, we will be able to take it in, that violence, hold it in our
hands . . . And the ones who come after us, maybe they can
understand us; forgive us; as we forgive our parents, our
grandparents, moving so distantly through their lives . . . their
silences . . .
And the ones we were with   maybe our friendship can change,
can mend . . .

Come stay here. Things change . . .

She stays home;

Not to invade   Wait, here, in the quiet

Lines from a Story

> *I remembered . . . [my grandfather] said that if you let your blood*
> *run, you make yourself better. If there are spirits in you that*
> *want to go, they will leave with the blood.*
> —An Eskimo woman, to Robert Coles

Mother   your quiet face
already at eight years old a survivor's face:

You say   there is no mother or father,
say, fear,   It is too cold
here, you say, I am alive,   I will
hold myself in my own hands.

The white beach in that photograph, white
lake, white sky, a page . . .   your story
that I know in such spent outlines . . .

But still your hands
hold me to you, here,
your voice reads to me, still,
—your voice that forgot itself
in other people's words—

You never thought you knew things.

And I have begun, so late, to trust what I love!
To hope
to gather in the rest.
Or let it go:
I cut my arm, it bled;
a long dawn
opening to here:

in my own hands
in the quiet   listening
—I send this page to you,
from memory:
lines from a story, about two friends
who lived in distant towns:
"—If I could talk to you now,
I believe we could be so simple,
if you could talk to me,
then we could be so still."

March 21st

*Out of 92 natural elements, we could never have predicted man. We
could never even get to the wetness of water, the miracle of ordinary
water. Water is one of the strangest substances in all of chemistry.*
—George Wald

5 a.m.

Waking. Something, dry, without shape, moving toward the tilted
faces, the voices, of the dream,

The room the clearing in the trees moving

Now, the thumbed line of daylight, behind them,
finding the room,　　　its lines, down, across—
my body　　　finding again　　　"I"

The words from a dream of yours, twenty years ago,
"Relay locality"

And you, my father, my brother, your face in my dream, receding,
your voice saying, what they told me you did say,
—*They're getting farther away; but it isn't them, it's me; I'm
getting old;*

Your voice, leaving:　　　and still the day

And you, my brother,
—*No wonder for the shame.*

And you, my mother, my sister,
our talk　　　our stillness　　　now

And you, my father, my mother,
"unlosable friend"

saying again
—*Here is the life outside the window,
　here is the earth, the water, here is
　fire, the blood, the breath moving through your own hands:*

　your work　　　*everyone you love*

And you, my sister, writing,
the hidden way of each of us, buried
To drift　　　allowing

forgetting my name　　　my life

the salt of our hands
touching

changing:

over and over: following

you   who I don't know
listening: changing

the play of the breath of the world

they   he   she   you

Home.Deep.B

1989

Willi, Home

in memory

Last night, just before sleep, this: a bright
daffodil
lying in bed, with the sheet pulled up to its chin.
Willi, did I ever know you? The shine
in the lamplight!   of your intelligent glasses,
round and humorous.
Did I ever know myself? When I
start bullshitting I see your eyebrows fly . . . This book
is dedicated to Willi,
whom I do not know,

whom I know. The words in my head
this morning
(these words came from an angel):
"It's too late to say goodbye.
And there are never enough goodbyes."
I know: the daffodil
is me. Brave. Willi's an iris. Brave.
Brave. Tall. Home. Deep. Blue.

To Raphael, angel of happy meeting

The pear tree buds shine like salt;
the stretch of new-ploughed earth holds up
five colors of brown to the strict sun—
like an old woman's open hand, at rest.

The young people of this house wake up,
one by one, they set out . . .

Further away, still their voices hold,
across the fog; and the pull of the ropes
—these branches rubbing in the rain—

Further away, the full sails   grains of salt
thrown into the wind . . .

The pear tree prints its buds
across my back, my hands,
bright drops of light, in the wind. Light,

Break through this husk, this
mask of 'Goodbye' . . .

Why was I crying?   It was as if
some courteous hand
had touched my eyes, and I saw,

in that thin Sixties backyard
in Seattle, the abundant tree
open out its branches, white-gold wings
protective of our waiting,
of our wishes, still too light for us to hold.

Primitive Painting: Liberation Day

Everyone is wearing work clothes, old clothes, boots; and old uni-
forms, painted green and brown, like trees. The new government has
asked everyone to assemble in the center of the Old City, and has
given everyone small ribbons to wear, stiff flowers.

Two men in business suits are pouring wine into cups, at a long trestle
table; a few of the men and women have begun to drink.

Home.Deep.Blue (1989) | 165

At the bottom corner of the painting is a row of bright green leaves,
like a signature. A tall man, in the foreground, looks straight out into
the painter's eyes; his hands are crossed over his genitals. There are no
children, or animals, in this picture; no one makes a sound, or has
another side.

This is a desert, and they call it peace, this is Liberation Day; the
new government is drunk again, and the painter's fear is white in his
paint.

Awake, This Summer

I see you a minute, a year ago, at the door
of our friend's empty room,
your eyes, the slanted-back weight of your body,

moseying around. That night, your hand
jumped in your sleep, you said
"Everyone was friends" . . .

Late summer mornings
I slept in your side, in the sun,
and to all your wishes in my sleep I wished "Yes."

A year's ocean of sleep we moved in,
without air; no one
was friends.

    Awake, this summer, first
finished with that, my chest hurts, and
the shallowest breath is life.

Mandelstam

*1934-35. The time of his arrest and imprisonment in Moscow,
and his exile, with his wife Nadezhda Jakolevna Khazina, to
Voronezh.*

My mother's house
Russia

Calm are the wolf's bronze udders,
calm the light around her
fur, out-starred with frost

I am 43
Moscow we will not live

Russia
Iron shoe
its little
incurved length and width

Russia   old
root cellar   old mouth of
blood under-the-earth
pulling us down into herself
no room to lie down

    and your poor hand
    over and over
    draws my brain
    back to your breast's small
    campfire

Voronezh we won't live
    not even my hand
    to hold to your hand, useless.

Home.Deep.Blue (1989) | **167**

The Drinker's Wife Writes Back

You never hear me, your letter said.
But I was the one who always listened
and understood, reliable, listening
at your thought's door . . . I was steady
as the oak our bed is made of . . .

The name of a good doctor, your letter said.
I wait in his green waiting room;
my hands are big, pale, idle, Neutral, intent,
his secretary calls me 'Dear,'
like one of my own children.

He is kind. I can't last out the hour.
The window panes behind him stare me down,
the lenses over his eyes. He asks, What brings me here?
But I feel—not naked—
but absent, made of air

because how could I ever have told
anyone how it was, how the lighted house
went out in the gin brightness
you called 'the war'—and that I did this to you—
I did not do this . . .

Birthday Letter from South Carolina
for Sarah, 21

Yellow apple
star inside the apple
seed star   quiet

Walking up this quiet, red-earth road,
I think of you there, near the white-
edged harbor; in a yellow kerchief,
in the blowing sunlight, you walk
along the concrete of the holding world.

You hold it all to your chest, the blue day, night,
long reading, long talk,   —You hold
your kind, stumbling, sure
life in your hands.
Indian cloth, the goose-neck desk light . . .

Basho spent the first thirty years of his life
apprenticing; four years alone in a small hut
on the outskirts of Tokyo;
the last ten years
walking. Walking here

today I saw him, Basho, at the far edge of the field;
and you alongside him; your steps,
his long black and white steps stirring up
red mica dust to drift across the new day's light, and the heat.

The Counselor Retires, and Then He Dies

Getting each other's jokes,
each other's absences; my first wise
practice at intimacy; and now the hero
shrugs on his London raincoat and walks away,
down the shiny street: it's a death, Doc.

No more of
you in your pale green office, your bright green pants,

your lounging, affectionate smile, you
cradling your dog when he had a cold,
the way you would cradle me, if I was a dog,
or a baby, the way God cradles us,
only we can't feel it . . .

Shea,
guard me and keep me,
as I keep you;
let me go, and I
let you go: a white balloon magic-markered *Shea*
floating up the white sky.

Juliana

Our lives went differently,
we lost touch . . .

The table is solid,
its long cloth shines.
Husband and wife lived in one house, forever,
and this was nothing wonderful, a simple fact.
Grown children gather, they bring
white tulips, forsythia.

All the guests make toasts. Sex taps at our sleeping ears
like water in another room . . .

The couples lean back, rich canvases. My hunger plays
in front of them, empty,—dozes off, day-dreaming
of true desire.
I try waking, try saying,

Well, we're all human,

> —One outlying face smiles
and leans forward, gray and mild . . .

Later Juliana
I meet you, a minute, on the stairs,
and you stop, and hold my arms,
and tears run down your face . . .

Just waking up
she didn't remember what time of year it was,
and couldn't remember if she had a friend
in the world, Oh thank God, summer, and she remembered last night
her husband's friend, the professor,
that he said, Waiting is what we do, in this life, we wait.

Visit

This warm house, masculine; our old,
20-years-old hug;
your gray eyes, that I trust.
But our clear,
perfect sentences,
like money. No silences.

Jokes, books, our friends . . .
Why are you always
the older one? Why am I
a wooden girl, not
friends when we meet?

> The other one, tough, dumb,
> kind, the monologuer,
> the strange one, with no house
> —after our first fight

we didn't have to have that fight anymore,
or go away.

Solid perfect waves
break in and pull back.

It was as if you shouted after me,
"Can't you see my death, can't you see anything?"

Snow Landscape, in a Glass Globe
in memory of Elizabeth Bishop

A thumb's-length landscape: Snow, on a hill
in China. I turn the glass ball over in my hand,
and watch the snow
blow around the Chinese woman,
calm at her work,
carrying her heavy yoke
uphill, towards the distant house.
Looking out through the thick glass ball
she would see the lines of my hand,
unearthly winter trees, unmoving, behind the snow . . .

No more elders.
The Boston snow grays and softens
the streets where you were . . .
Trees older than you, alive.

The snow is over and the sky is light.
Pale, pale blue distance . . .
Is there an east? A west? A river?
There, can we live right?

I look back in through the glass. You,
in China, I can talk to you.
The snow has settled; but it's cold
there, where you are.

What are you carrying?
For the sake of what? through such hard wind
and light.
       —And you look out to me,
and you say, "Only the same as everyone; your breath,
your words, move with mine,
under and over this glass; we who were born
and lived on the living earth."

Everything Starts with a Letter

Everything starts with a letter,
even in dreams and in the movies ... Take
J. Juliana, on a summer afternoon,
in a white silk blouse, and a pale blue-flowered skirt,
—her shoes? blue? but high and narrow heels,
because she asks Sam to carry the plate of Triscuits
into the garden, because she can't manage
the brick path in her heels.
"Oh could you? I can't manage the path in these heels."

J is the letter my name begins with,
O is the letter for the moon,
and my rage shines in my throat like the moon!
Her phoniness, O my double, your and
my phoniness . . .
Now what shall we do?
For this is how women begin to shoot,
we begin with our own feet, men empty their hearts, oh

the false self will do much worse than that,
to get away . . .

About Love

1
No   when you went to her
(oh when she told me so) then I turned to
her   her   her   her: emptiness:

black hollows falling over alone
under the white running water

2
"Light as milk in a child's cup,
I will hold you, at my lips
I will feed you," said the soft black pelican
about love, the mother, God the pelican,
the mother, stem of all our tenderness.

3
Ribbon of the
silver path of the milky
light on the water, how
you follow yourself across my mouth,
across my hair;

beads of water,
bright tall necklace of light, how you
thread yourself through me, through
my lips, their silk
stem.

174 | *Light Me Down: The New & Collected Poems of Jean Valentine*

Little Song in Indian Summer

I am
is my name and your name, *I am* is
the name we are finding,
I am is the
name who is finding us, is
(standing still in the high grass, in the hot sun)
the one I always wanted to find, is
the one I always wanted to find,
not mother, not child, oh you
I need
who are glad
I am I
with your green eyes even
with welcome, with letting go.

The King

You take the card of your self out
at the green crossroads, you
pull your name close around you.
But whose words are you speaking? Whose
money is this? Your warm
mouth on my mouth stuns me, your hand
on my breast is so bright, I
have to shut my eyes . . .

Still I won't take the card you offer,
though its coin is highly prized,
and its coin is wild,
—its coin is "Mine be mine,"
its coin is "And I will love you then,"
its coin was death

Home.Deep.Blue (1989) | 175

to the thirsty child
not heard but drowned in the deep sea ...

High School Boyfriend

You were willing to like me, and I did something,
and blew it,
and your liking me would have saved me,
and my liking you would have saved you,

that was the circle I was walking around,
pushing a bar that moved a wheel
down in the dark, holding my breath,
naked in a long hard army coat of you,
hating my feet, hating my path ...

Today my tongue is a fish's tongue,
kissing my friend's light breastbone, his chestnut down;
full of tears, full of light, half both,
nowhere near my old home: no one anywhere
is so wrong.

Tonight I Can Write.
after Pablo Neruda

Tonight I can write the lightest lines.

Write, for example, 'The evening is warm
and the white mist holds our houses close.'

The little evening wind walks in the field grass
and hums into her own chest.

Tonight I can write the lightest lines.
I love him, and I think he loves me too.

He first came to me on an evening like this one
and held me in his arms.

He kissed me again and again then,
under the motherly bending down stars.

He loves me, and I think I love him too.
How could one not love his calm eyes, as blue as the earth.

Tonight I can write the lightest lines.
To think that I did not know him, that now I am beginning to know him.

To feel the warm lamplight: soon it will warm his brown arm
'And the verse falls to the soul like dew to the pasture . . .'

Trust Me

Who did I write last night? leaning
over this yellow pad, here, inside,
making blue chicken tracks: two
sets of blue footprints, tracking out
on a yellow ground,
child's colors.

Who am I?
who want so much to move
like a fish through water,
through life . . .

Fish *like* to be
underwater.

Fish move through fish! Who
are you?

And Trust Me said, There's another way to go,
we'll go by the river which is frozen under the snow;

my shining, your shining life draws close, draws closer,
God fills us as a woman fills a pitcher.

The River at Wolf

1992

To the memory of my mother
Jean Purcell Valentine
and to Barrie Cooke

X

I have decorated this banner to honor my brother. Our parents did not want his name used publicly.
—from an unnamed child's banner in the AIDS Memorial Quilt.

The boatpond, broken off, looks back at the sky.
I remember looking at you, X, this way,
taking in your red hair, your eyes' light, and I miss you
so. I know,
you are you, and real, standing there in the doorway,
whether dead or whether living, real. —Then Y
said, "Who will remember me three years after I die?
What is there for my eye
to read then?"
The lamb should not have given
his wool.
He was so small. At the end, X, you were so small.
Playing with a stone
on your bedspread at the edge of the ocean.

Spring and Its Flowers

Then, *Tell me your fantasies,* you said.
And I: *OK; I'm lying in bed, asleep, a child,*
and you, you're sitting in the rocker there, knitting,
like a mother bear. And you:
Can I be the one in the bed, too?
And you in the chair there, knitting?

That February you dreamed your old father said, *Spring*
this year and its flowers
will cost you eighteen thousand dollars.
Waking up we wished we could have lived together
in a green and blue walled garden forever...

We didn't know
we were so close
to the world's mouth, the drunk bear's ashy thing.

The Summer Was Not Long Enough

Stanley, my ex, the painter,
stepped out of his van.
His beard was gone. Loudly, carefully,
he started to paint the trees
and the ground and the telephone poles
grass green.

Funny, I was crying
after him: not Stan's upsidedown-ness,
my own. My own friends, not written back,
not called. Oh our love
turned from, and August half over.

August's more than half over;
Dove, it's time for peace.
Time to taste the round mountains, the white and green,
and the dusk rose of relationship, again,
for the first time, it's time to take off our clothes,
and the fortresses around our eyes, to touch our first fingers,
you and I, like God, across everything.

The River at Wolf (1992) | **183**

Still Life, for Matisse

Light
old leaf spine
fish spine bone
green under-the-
ocean light
big gold fish my
new little father
only a boy
breathing on the window
COME ON OUT
you carry me I carry you
light wave after wave
swim cockatoo
green, blue.

Still Life: in the Epidemic

Light
old leaf spine
fish spine bone
green under-the-
ocean light

big gold fish my
new little father
only a boy
breathing on the window
COME ON OUT,

my eggful of eggs
floating opening
up in your cream, up in

your blood,
Are you sick? Are you well?

A blood sample will be taken from your
arm with a needle and analyzed in a
laboratory using a test called ELISA
(enzyme-linked immunosorbent assay).
If the ELISA test is positive, a
second test, called Western Blot, will
be run on the same blood sample to
confirm the result.

The palm of your glove is
powder on my mouth, powder in my fear,
your rough tongue your talk
is warm on the cool hospital issue
black silk blindfold crackhouse blindfold

you green in the dark tying a rubber
strap around my arm playing the radio
your heavy head, green in the dark.
Are you still in the room?
Are you still in the house?

Then you, Doctor,
you say sincerely,
"You can always go on suicide neutral,
then everyone, from both sides, from his side and her side,
will leave you alone." And Mother

State, you say, "You are not enough.
I am. Eat me, and
I will raise you up. On TV, eat me.
Chew me, gingerly, like chewing ice,
eat me. America. Eat me."

The River at Wolf (1992) | **185**

Ikon

Swim in you, sleep
in you, let me,
Mother Lord,
all this hour

—I am your cloth of gold
swaddled firstchild
safe in danger
(you are in danger)

one hand curled around your
bending neck, the other
rested on your black breast,
just above your star.

Winter in the world
is winter here in you
but summer, too,

oh my play,
my eyes, my light. Black
hill of consolation! There is no book
and my name is written in it, my heart makes
an earth crib for your heart.

The Year of the Snake

I had to ask you questions: if I didn't, well
you'd think I'd robbed a bank. And then, blood all over, God,
I would've robbed a bank. But my old God,
my questions were too small for you. You
were so much older, you *knew* so much. You

used your words like bricks, whole leathery old
books black with words, to wall me out, words gold
as booze, to leave the room, leave me, leave us. Oh
since that time, I have learned
to let you go and live...

Now my friend happy as God I sit down and comb your hair.
Your hair shines like honey like sex like the current in the river.
The river combs out our anger our tenderness.
Our silent tenderness not *my* or *mine* or *yours*.
Your unspeaking mouth shining.
Shining lifesnake drinking at my lips milky with life.

The One You Wanted to Be Is the One You Are

She saying, You don't have to do anything,
you don't even have to be, you Only who are,
you nobody from nowhere,
without one sin or one good quality,
without one book, without one word,
without even a comb, you!
The one you wanted to be
is the one you are. Come play...

And he saying,
Look at me!
I don't know how...

Their breath like a tree's breath. Their silence
like a deer's silence. Tolstoy
wrote about this: all misunderstanding.

The River at Wolf (1992) | **187**

Ironwood

November 17th
Dear Michael,

I had gotten *Ironwood, The Final Issue*, in the mail; I put it on
the table, and lay down to sleep, and dreamed I was talking to
you. You said, "You're much younger than my mother, of
course, but you look like her." You said, "I'm going to kill
myself." And I said, "How does your mother feel about that?"
You said, "She's without feelings, very factual; she says, There's
only a fifty-fifty chance you'll pull it off with this method, they're
so good these days at reviving people with money." "What
method, Michael?" And you said, "The broth method." Then
you said, "Did you imagine, when you were a youngster, that in
30 or 40 years you would be my mother, and having this conver-
sation?" I said, "That's right, it *is* 30, no, 40 years. I don't want to
be in your mother's shoes right now."

Waking up, I thought: No, this is the other Michael.

Bud

Christmas night, my father said, "Jean,
you are so disloyal." But Bud said,
"No. Ethereal. Ethereal, but my friend.
And I, I *got* my prayer answered:
I died with my life around me."

To a Young Poet
for Michael Klein

This January night at ten below I wish you
true desire, like a rose: to stand
in your chest. Veined. Bloom.

Let you be. Reflected in the train window,
inside a thousand circles of public darkness,
desire, a round red star.

And desire again, a foliating wand,
and you the Jack of Wands.

The round red rose of sleep in bloom. This is
true desire, it lets you be.
It says, "No money here."

What does it taste like?
True desire. Eye-
shadow, cinnamon.

Foraging

1. The Room

Why did you keep finding me where I was?
Your seeking, your cage:
oh, your animus against breasts, shadowed eyelids...
yet like holding your breath, holding Love.

Love, you said,
come in. Love, let me in.
Everyone else was asleep.
Look at me, you said.

The River at Wolf (1992) | **189**

The luminous room.
Eve formalized.

A kiss: my fear and
my love,

not here yet,
but *for* here.

2. *The Luminous Room*

What it felt like:
first it was the kiss.
Look at me, he said.
And then it was the floor,
the boards. He went slow, he'd
pull and pull and pull at my leaf thirst.

Or running backwards he'd wind the kite-string lace
down out of me so the hot slow wind
would almost touch me... No... Then Jesus God,
the first room: sky, and trees,
but water: blue blue blue bloom bloom.
It was the feeling of terrible scarcity
and then it was the boards
and then it was the luminous room.

Alfred and the Abortion

Alfred, what did they do with your arm bones?
Burned, lying in ashes and clinkers,

or long arm bones lying inwards
Christian-folded fallen across your dropped
rib bones, out there on Long Island...

Your heavy right wrist bones
that engineered your work:
a rose, a rainbow of oil on the rowboat floor:

the baby we lost in sixty-nine, with you
in the hospital out of work when I did it
and I couldn't have told you then. Her name was Gift.

Twenty years later I dreamed last night of your wrist,
me eating your wrist, for the child to eat it,
your hand working, and the virtue of your wrist.

Redemption

for James Chace

Nan, the poet in Rome, New York, yesterday
wrote she saw the word "Confluence" in her sleep.

The run of black hair down your arm,
in the deep-worn line across your polished shoe.

"Confluence": two rivers joining,
or, the longing to return:

because Jim, we parted
on either side of this green island,
Christ! It seems it was a hundred years ago.

But now there is no inside wall:
all down our bodies, from our heads to our feet,

The River at Wolf (1992) | 191

there's only a line like light,
and all around us
a line like an eggshell of light.

Seeing You

1. Mother

I was born under the mudbank
and you gave me your boat.

For a long time
I made my home in your hand:

your hand was empty, it was made
of four stars, like a kite;

you were afraid, afraid, afraid, afraid,
I licked it from your finger-spaces

and wanted to die.
Out of the river sparks rose up:

I could see you, your fear and your love.
I could see you, brilliance magnified.

That was the original garden:
seeing you.

2. Lover

Your hand was empty. It was made
of four stars, like a kite;

blessed I stood my fingers
in your blue finger-spaces, my eyes' light in

your eyes' light,
we drank each other in.

I dove down my mental lake fear and love:
first fear then under it love:

I could see you,
Brilliance, at the bottom. Trust you

stillness in the last red inside place.
Then past the middle of the earth it got light again.

Your tree. Its heavy green sway. The bright male city.
Oh that was the garden of abundance, seeing you.

The Free Abandonment Blues

Now I don't have to leave this place not for anybody
No I don't have to go out of this wooden house not to oblige
    anybody
Once I would have lifted clean out of my own place to please
    somebody

The blue-robed man who said You want to be loved, love me
The man in the blue robe who said I give, in order that you will
    give to me
I remember you my old blue-robed man, but you know this just
    can not be

Now if I want to warm myself I look up at the blue sky
Now I look to a number of people here and also to the round blue

sky
To feel the sun, your free mouth on my mouth, not the fire that is
    gone by

I don't wear any clothes nowadays or say that I am me
I don't wear the right clothes in the closet or explain how I am me
I come as I go translucent oh what you get is what you see

The woman said:
They held her in their arms and knew that she would save them
They brought her into their houses and into their hands to save
    them
But secretly they knew that no one would ever have them

And she said,
Listen, it's only a little time longer to wait
When you have taken this path you need just a little more time to
    wait
maybe not today the amazing loveliness but it won't be long for
    us to wait

The First Station

The first silver work of kindness,
my hand, your hand and your eye, and then the gold play
of watery car lights across the child's white quilt
we slept under and on top of, that February. . .

The rude walnut smell of the hibernation nest.
Sleeping I thought

If there was a hole through you
and a hole through me
they'd take the same

peg or needle
and thread us both
through the first station
and there we'd lean
and listen and listen. . .

Night Lake

He must have been one or two, I was five,
my brother Johnny's cock
floated like a rose of soap in the tub;
it had the faint, light rock of the boat
you carry in you when you're on land again
at the end of the day. . .

Oh all I've never gotten written down!
On paper, on my skin. Oh navy blue lake
that I want to drink
to the bottom. And you,
Barrie, what can I give you to drink?
Not the flask of ourselves, we already have that.

The solitude drink
in the kerosene lamplight at the caravan table. . .

The River at Wolf (1992) | 195

The Badlands Said

I am the skull
under your hundred doubts. I, I
will be with you always.
Heart's-deprive.
Still numinous and alive.
Elephant's side.

Come lie down,
tooth and bone.

Ya, ya,
from a mile high
I crook you up warm,
rabbit-arm.

I am love's sorrow,
the desert's violet needle and gray star.

The Missouri Speaks

> *for Jonathan Dunn, 1954-1988*
> *Wolf Creek, Montana*

Jonathan,
I am the pearl
The pearl at the node of the net of all the worlds

The jewel at the crown of your head
Turquoise

Ivory embryo
Spiral I bide

Sow and reap
Bale and step

Sow bread
Reap bread

Powerless I promise
Fire and bones and flesh

All I give I will sheave.

The River at Wolf

Coming east we left the animals
pelican beaver osprey muskrat and snake
their hair and skin and feathers
their eyes in the dark: red and green.
Your finger drawing my mouth.

Blessed are they who remember
that what they now have they once longed for.

A day a year ago last summer
God filled me with himself, like gold, inside,
deeper inside than marrow.

This close to God this close to you:
walking into the river at Wolf with
the animals. The snake's
green skin, lit from inside. Our second life.

The River at Wolf (1992) | **197**

The Ring

The ring was
three times too small for a finger,
even a piece of string could not go through it!
So I asked her,
Woman, why have you sold or given me this ring?
Nunlike she bobbed her white head-scarf chastisingly,
black eyes, black under her eyes, she said,
Something is being taken away.
You must keep seeing: everything
must be turned to love that is not love.
Mother,
going in to death,
can you do it: love
something that was there that is being taken away.

Barrie's Dream, the Wild Geese

"I dreamed about Elizabeth Bishop
and Robert Lowell—an old Penguin book
of Bishop's poetry—a thick china cup
and a thick china sugar bowl, square,
cream-colored, school stuff.

               And Lowell was there,
he was talking and talking to us,
he was saying, 'She is the best—'
Then the geese flew over,
and he stopped talking. Everyone stopped talking,
because of the geese."

              The sounds of their wings!
Oars rowing, laborious, wood against wood: it was
a continuing thought, no, it was a labor,
how to accept your lover's love. Who could do it alone?
Under our radiant sleep they were bearing us all night long.

Fox Glacier

The Tourist: Blue plough bones
                      High eye socket
                      Soot rock gristle
                      Be with me
                      Be with me
                      Be with me
                      Never be not with us
                      Fox

The Glacier: My gentle coming: fall
                      I am with you my
                      Gold-pan
                      My sieved and sieving brow
                      Most wanted: Favorite:
                      Wanted and needed and loved: Diaspora.

Lindis Pass, Borage

in memory of Patricia Walsh

Mary
when you swam up (in reality rose,
assumed) to feed on bliss:
that rounder reality:
you left your dress blue borage like a painted dress
permanent violet cobalt ultramarine and white
lighting this chainlink gate;

open for Pat:
ten children, emphysema, dead at forty:
"Too good for this world."

The River at Wolf (1992) | 199

Open for me! I slam against the gate
dumber than any sheep. I want, I want.
I want to become round like you there: like God: reality:
not flat like here, all oil, all pleasantness and heat.

By the Tekapo River, 100 Degrees

Water
Hot green plastic bucket
Hole
Rabbit in the wall of the ground
Bone
Rabbit, hip, shoulder
Leaf   under a leaf of dust

On my way to wash,
the heavy buzz of flies like bees:
there's a carcass here. Rabbit. Eels
live to be ninety... An eel will eat your hand.

I smell the past: where you swam with me,
not toothed as you are, but as you were,
safe in your first, soft shirt.

After Consciousness of This Big Form

Sam and I chose a workshop called
"Fruitfulness." At the round door
a beautiful leader met us, smiling.
Many people pooled into the room,
they opened their arms and they rolled their heads around,

like an old musical, opened their arms and rolled their heads
   around:

"When I get up in the morning,
after consciousness of this big form..."

Maybe so-and-so would like a child,
but I am too old to give birth. Too old,
too much wanting to live my life, not take care
of anyone as so-and-so takes of so-and-so.
When I get up in the morning I am water and wine
with this big form, this pouring out spiral of stars...

Everyone Was Drunk

South Dakota, August 1989. The buffaloes' deep red-brown
hinged shoulders and beards, their old hinged humps...
These are the old males, separated from the herd.
You can get a state license to shoot them.

"So who saved me? And for what purpose?"

The rich WASP suburb, 1946. The fight
about the Jews on Wall Street. My uncle said,
I thought that's what we fought the war about.
My uncle was right; everyone was drunk; my mother
was peeling shivers of Scotch tape off the counter, peeling off
her good hope. Or was it I who was losing my hope? in the
violent lightning white on the white lawn.
So why was I handed out of the burning window?
For joy. Journalism. Stories.

The River at Wolf (1992) | 201

In Fear (1)

By the St. Vrain River
thirty cars, thirty young men
looking down into the water.
What are they looking at? Now the police cars.
What is going to happen? Now the ambulances.
Someone was here and is gone.

In Fear (2)

M. comes and hits me,
along the spine,
top to bottom,
karate-handed.
I say, It hurts me! And she,
her face the face of a person
in Hell, compelled to unhappy action:
"It hurts everyone."

In This Egg

My mother as a child
under her father's sexual hand
ticking over her like an electric train.
The household scissors to her hair.

Scissors cut paper
Paper covers rock
Rock crushes scissors

Sticks and fluttering paper notes
gravestones   river stones
scissors   holocaust.

My mother and her father, in this blue egg.
This egg, our young, gone before us:
who will brood over them?
Who will make a good roof over them.

The Under Voice

I saw streaming up out of the sidewalk the homeless women and men
the East side of Broadway fruit and flowers and bourbon
the homeless men like dull knives grey-lipped the homeless women
connected to no one streaming no one to no one
more like light than like people, blue neon,
blue the most fugitive of all colors

Then I looked and saw our bodies
not near but not far out
lying together, our whiteness

And the under voice said, Stars you are mine,
you have always been mine; I remember the minute on the birth table
when you were born, I riding with my feet up in the wide silver-blue stirrups,
I came and came and came, little baby and woman, where were you taking me?
Everyone else may leave you, I will never leave you, fugitive.

The River at Wolf (1992) | **203**

Come Ahkmatova

A homeless woman with harsh white hair
stands outside my Chinese-red door
blocking my way into my
home place:
She says *I lived here once.*
This was my place. I want my pictures.

I have them, the glass of the frames is broken,
if she comes in
she will be my bad ikon,
throw me away
as I throw her away, her
gray unmoving accusing stare. Come Ahkmatova
in the siege of Leningrad:
"Can you write about this?" "I can."

James Wright: in Memory

Looking back at me
from his death, from the feminine side, he asks me
to touch him on his throat, on his breastbone,
to touch the spots that have the life in them. His voice
is closer to me than I am to myself.
Unknowable, beginning in joy, his voice
is closer to me than I am to myself.

Wish-Mother

I've never felt
so close to you, Wish-Mother. Wings, oh
my black darling. Almost free.
Never felt so close to anyone. Felt,
Hide you in the shelter of my wings.
All the way home to New York my heart hurt.
Am I taking the old glass out of the frame? Are we?

I love glass because of water,
water because of blood,
blood because of your heart,
lapping against the birth door to my ear,
over and over, my darling, my familiar. And my good.
All the way home to New York my heart hurt.
(The second time you died this year.)

At Cullens' Island

in memory of Eimear Cullen,
1983-1990

Eimear was dead:
Every rock was a green womb, lit from inside.
The trees were like big soft women
whose mossy hooves
burned at the touch of the earth:
Eimear was dead:
Every rock was a green womb, lit from inside.

The Wisdom Gravy

Goosedown on the warm curve of a pail.
Hundreds of young rooks flying into the tree.
John: *I'd like to get good at it, at being married.*
Me: *Well you can't do better than that.*
John: *She thinks I can do much better, than talk about wanting!*
I said to her, I know I haven't done well
these last two years, these first few years,
but I want to get good at it. I'm good at being alone.

A.'s jealousy. B.'s jealousy. Of life.
All night I sucked at wisdom like a shooting tooth:
this morning life's a light garment, a garment of light,
like in our paradise. A. keeps the manger, B. keeps it too, forever
and ever. This gravy is wide and deep, saltier and stranger,
I've carried it home to you under my white hat.

American River Sky Alcohol Father

What is pornography? What is dream?
American River Sky Alcohol Father,
forty years ago, four lifetimes ago,
brown as bourbon, warm, you said to me,
"Sorry sorry sorry sorry sorry."
Then: "You're killing your mother."
And she: "You're killing your father."
What do men want? What do fathers want?
Why won't they go to the mothers?
(What do the mothers want.)
American River Sky Alcohol Father,
your warm hand. Your glass. Your bedside table gun.
The dock, the water, the fragile, tough beach grass.
Your hand. I wouldn't swim. I wouldn't fly.

206 | *Light Me Down: The New & Collected Poems of Jean Valentine*

The Morning of My Mother's Death

A thumbnail-sized globe of blood:
an embryo:
I lose it, I can't find it.
A woman, a midwife or a companion,
says, do I *want* her to kill it?

Our mother wants to take herself
away from us. My kisses.
She loves another country
better than this.
Another class of people.
The class of the dead.

Listen listen listen:
(whisper this:)
her silk spirit is leaving the crown of her head.

The Night of My Mother's Death
for Richard McCann

The night of my mother's death:
what I saw:

They are winding a bandage all around her head. I say,
Leave holes for her eyes and her mouth.
Then I look down, and I see,
my own wrist is only a spine of bones.

Then how will I listen any more?

I ask you Davoren Hanna, and you say:
"Ordinary communication is too slow

The River at Wolf (1992) | 207

to succinctly indicate
my meaning."

I ask you Emily Dickinson,
water-spider rowing over danger and death: four white lines,
four white lines: nothing over nothing.

Second Mother

Black hair,
and the white hill,
and the one cedar tree, "like a soldier,"

the ripe hot stench of your motorcycle,
its squatting gleam...

Then, by the river,
Ha! Ha! I could have touched
your bright white circles,
your nipples' little red mouths
redder than my mother's

Black Hair, Black Hair! I was four, you were
sixteen, seventeen, half-girl, half-mother,
you held out safety like a sugar cube,
but how could I get to suck on it? in this world...

The Sea of Serenity

The Sea of Serenity:
my mother's body: ashes:
the appearance of land, and the appearance of water.

Books by the fireplace: gold brocade and silver:
but love, oh love. Outside the door.

Earth said, *Eat.*
Earth said, *Shame.*

Mother,
on my hands and knees,
face flat in the leaves,
I chomp after you like a horse.

Who died?
Who died?
Who died?

My Mother's Body, My Professor, My Bower

Who died? My mother's body,
my professor, my bower,
my giant clam.
Serene water, professor
of copious clay,
of spiraling finger-holes in the clay,
of blue breast-milk,
first pulse, all thought:
there is nothing to get. You can't eat money,
dear throat, dear longing,
dear belly, dear fatness,

The River at Wolf (1992) | 209

dear silky fastness: ecstatic lungs' breath,
you can't protect yourself,
there is nothing to get.

Butane

The huge aluminum airship
is gliding over us,
you and I with our children walking by Westport's
trees, seashore, gold trees, gold seashore.
I say, *What's that?* But no one sees it.
Then the second ship crashes just behind us,
spills butane lighter fluid over the field,
thinly spreading, fast, out over the next field;
we don't know, should we throw water over it
or not—which will be worse for the earth
(the earth itself isn't on fire yet,
only the corn in the field, and in the next field).
The dwarf says, *Hold it!* walking up between my legs
into my body: *I'd better see the fire skin.*

At My Mother's Grave

Being told,
Go away.

So what is left?
This dark space on the road, that was a deer.
So many gifts:
her hazel eyes. . .

What day did she go away?

Walt Whitman,
visitor,
Emily Dickinson,
canoe of light,
Pablo Neruda,
radio flier,
fly me in.

We Go Through Our Mother's Things

When we started that day
to paint snow for earth
and sky for bread
then we knew it was time to light the last candle.
This ring is yours. This lamp.

Death Asphodel

— I feel like I've buried somebody inside of me
    Parts of her
    I don't remember yet
    Parts of myself I don't remember yet

— Yes you mean
    there is somebody blind and gummy
    lying next to you when you're asleep

— Yes that's it. Goodbye,
    down the elevator,

something about flowers,
about giving flowers. Me
to my daughter?
My daughter to me?
My mother to me. Green flowers soon to bloom.

To the Memory of David Kalstone

Here's the letter I wrote,
and the ghost letter, underneath—
that's my work in life.

The First Angel

Fat slippery angels,
two by two,
carrying sheaves of straw
to the graveyard,
leaning sheaves of straw
on the gravestones,
straw on the frost stones.

God's hands trembled when he
touched my head,
we are so much in love:
the new moon holding the old moon in her arms.

The first angel said, Write down this:
It is time to leave your past life, leave your plumb-line, your trowel,
your layers of habitation, your perfect finds-tray.

At the Door

Seeing my daughter in the circle of lamplight,
I outside:

It is not *I*,
it is *Mother.*
(But it is *I*.)

It is the first tableau, the first
red wellspring of *I*.

Chimpanzee of longing,
outside the light,
wrap your long arms
around the globe of light,
hold your long haunches
wide open: be
ungodly I.

Yield Everything, Force Nothing

Years circling the same circle:
the call to be first,
and the underlying want:

and this morning, look! I've finished now,
with this terrific red thing,
with green and yellow rings on it, and stars.

The contest is over:
I turned away,
and I am beautiful: Job's last daughters,
Cinammon, Eyeshadow, Dove.

The River at Wolf (1992) | 213

The contest is over:
I let my hands fall,
and here is your garden:
Cinnamon. Eyeshadow. Dove.

Alone, Alive

Alone, alive
with you
more alone
more alive
open open
to and from
the bloodwarm breast
the nest you were born to
the eye the hair
the window the light. Light
the astronauts saw
and grew full of trepidation,
softer,
and more full of life.

My window
my cove
my trout
my flood
my green trepidation
my mushroom
my tongue
my salt my moon
my moon my sun
I lay down my
spear
before your light

your eye
your hair.

Flower

You, I, steadying
in our in-borne, out-borne sparks
of empathy, the flower
of Earth: wet red fireworks-flower.

Skate

Now a year after your death, fish-mother, skate,
you swim up off the surface of the earth:
your other-worldly face
not saying anything
face I can never meet
inside the inside face
not since the land came wet
out of the water, face
under all the pieces of light,
how could I get to you?
Never leave you. Please you!
Teacher, spine in my spine:
the spelling of the world
kneels down before the skate.

The River at Wolf (1992) | **215**

Guardian Angel in New York

You stood in the doorway in the snow:
Times Square, a late hour.
The sill was black with chicken's blood:
your black boots open: your glasses like O's:
you touched your finger to your lips, you said,
Here: Wisdom. Wisdom and power.

To Plath, to Sexton

So what use was poetry
to a white empty house?

Wolf, swan, hare,
in by the fire.

And when your tree
crashed through your house,

what use then
was all your power?

It was the use of you.
It was the flower.

The Power Table

You, lying across the wide bed, vertical,
I, horizontal,

you, I, in a green field two green paths
flowered with xxxx's and xxxx's

you, I, lined inside
with pre-historic quarrels

old black cuts
in a wooden kitchen table

the table where you sit down with your older brothers
the table where things get settled once & for all

the cow's hip shaved down to the brand
her body divided into zones

Yes I am standing in the doorway
yes my softness & my hardness are filled with a secret light,

but I want world-light
and this-world company.

Growing Darkness, Growing Light

1997

I . . . like to deal with the relationship between growing darkness and growing light, the dusk and the dawn, those times when there is a chance to see transition . . . The dream is a connection, another transitional time. An example would be light coming into the world at dawn. In dreams we sometimes can see resemblances of where we really came from, whether we can explain it or not.

—Lance Henson, in Joseph Bruchac's *Survival This Way,*
Interviews with American Indian Poets

Growing Darkness, Growing Light (1997) | **221**

Rain

Snakes of water and light in the window
snakes that shrug out of their skins and follow
pushing a part with their heads full of light
—heavy trembling mercury headlights—
leaving trails of clear grass, and rocks,
nests where they half live, half sleep,
above ground:
Snake where do you come from?
who leave your grass path
and follow me wordless
into our glass
water and light house,
earth wet on your mouth,
you the ground of my underground.

Sick, Away from Home

My head
the Jenny Lind's head,
the painted tall ship's figurehead:
full, staring eyes,
beautiful:
but instead of the prow's wood at her back,
at my back a Monarch wing,

and the head and the wing
held up not by her wooden neck
and breasts of wood
but by an upright, silent thumb;
dream thumb
                    —me dreaming
over the wet electric New York streets.

Friend

Friend I need your hand every morning
but anger and beauty and hope
these roses make one rose.

Friend I need a hand every evening
but anger and hope and beauty
are three roses
that make one rose.

Let's fix our bed it's in splinters
and I want to stay all year.

Let's fix our bed it's in splinters
and I want to stay all year.

Did you hear what that woman on Grafton Street was saying?

You won't be killed today.
We don't even know we're born.

Homesick

Leonardo's man in the circle, but a woman,
the circle adrift in the middle of the lake:
cross through the line someone, salmon or hawk.

The rowboat drifts
on this northern evening's midnight line of light,
green lip reflecting lip,
and I float in it,
salt, and breath, and light,
hawk and salmon and I . . .

Growing Darkness, Growing Light (1997) | **223**

New Life

B. walks around with a fire-box inside his chest.
If you get near him it will burn you too. B. says

Don't let the women go out of our lives like the swallows
leaving only the crows' liquid leathery reign, domain, stain.

I love B.   And I love my life.
The taste of my own life is good to me. New life.
My skin.   And B.'s fire skin.

Bees

A man whose arms and shoulders
and hands and face and ears are covered with bees
says, *I've never known such pain.*
Another man comes over
with bees all over his hands—
only bees can get the other bees off.
The first man says again,
I've never known such pain.
The second man's bees begin to pluck
the first grave yellow bees off, one by one.

The Tractors

The tractors at night,
the dimly lighted
kindly lobsters
with glass sides,

with men inside,
and at home, wives,
and depression's black dogs
walking out of
the January hedges'
hacked-off sides.

River Jordan

O mud mother lick me before I die
before I'm only
a wooden case of disintegration
disowned things

and then—after this life—
the scar part, the lily, the rose *not* descending?
the eagle above the Wyoming
road? with six-foot wings outspread . . .

—No, not your mother either, this is me
the one who kissed you on your lips, your
nose, your stomach (secretly!), who carried you, it's me
who you belong to in reality.

Night Porch

Back home, after a month away
leaning on my night porch

what had I come to? out of air,
nose at the glass: to this gold dress

Growing Darkness, Growing Light (1997) | **225**

Nose at the glass: sweet inside world
where there was enough, enough, enough

And here was my husband
the grazer-beside, the distance sharer

but not he, or I, but the inside angel
held open the glass door, and led us led us . . .

*

World-light

Do well in the world.

If you do well
we'll throw you away.

We'll put you in the state asylum
like we did your grandfather.

(He did well then fell.)
("The drink." "But harmless.")
    But if you fall

we'll never say your name.
They'll think you're dead.

You will be one of the
Disappeared.

(We too, although we live
on a certain street, have certain jobs,

we too, we were
the Neverhere.)

Snow Family

Snow family: big snow father,
coal eyes, coal teeth,

small snow mother, no mouth,
smaller and smaller snow daughters,

and over them, a red felt banner:
I LIKE MY WOMEN'S VOICES SOFT.

And who were the child wife, husband, Mother
Father? King Queen? Brother? Never

to know. The snow
streamed upward
into the scree . . .

To the Black Madonna of Chartres

Friend or no friend,
darkness or light,
vowels or consonants,
water or dry land,
anything more from you now
is just gravy
—just send me down forgiveness, send me down
bearing myself a black cupful of light.

Growing Darkness, Growing Light (1997) | **227**

Tell Me, What Is the Soul

There is a prison room,
the floor, cement,
in the middle of the room
a black pool full of black water.
It leads to an invisible canal.
Plunder is the pool. Plunder is the canal.

By the wall,
by a fire,
Mandelstam was reciting,
in his yellow leather coat,
the criminals were listening,
they offered him
bread and the canned stuff,
which he took ...

Mastectomy
for Maura

They used to make a new breast for you
—no you made it: for who, for who—
with a bag of birdseed.

What happened to your breast?
No good to eat,
no good for love,
hungry hungry.

In a forest fire you make a fire
the size of yourself,
let it go out,
and lie in it.

I am hungry for my own heart. Heart's
work is normal harsh and sweet: throw out the
hospital bracelet, the hiding sheet.

Secret Room, Danger House

—Secret Room, Danger House:
the place where my belly
and my bone shelf meet:

Secret Room, Danger House:
dirty red inside:

—No it's clear, ruby red,
red as this ring
I give thee love.

Red for Blood

My sister comes around the corner of the house
carrying two bloody lambs, new-born
or hurt, I don't know, Eternity,
they beam blood.

They beam blood.
A little boy
comes down the chimney to bring me back
up with him. Covered with soot.

I don't want to go,
but I can't not go,

Growing Darkness, Growing Light (1997) | **229**

the animals all
go up like chimney-sweeps, Eternity,
you, me, up on a rope like the live geese,
chimney-sweep geese.

Yellow for Gold

Begging my mother to speak to him,
I pleaded my silent father's cause.

I pleaded my cause with my daughter.
My my my
my baby my Solomon also.

I bought a coconut boat
from a Rastafarian man: he said,
This boat is red for blood,
yellow for gold, green for the land,
black for the people.

Nightbook, nightboat of lights.

Where does my gold come from,
Solomon? Freely given, freely
taken away. Fly, father, daughter, fly.

Green for the Land

Because why—I was dis-
similar—

they staked my feet,
tied my hands,
threw me in,
but I stuck, I
caught on the side,
they see:
I lived.

No more room on the pages
of my green book to write on,
and someone coming back
wanting me: thief
of my land, my childhood thief.

Black for the People

The man I am with is black,
we are with nothing but white men.
He's caught, he says
they're going to shock him or burn him.
I say I'll be there.

But I'm not him.
He has to go into a machine where
two white men put him. The machine
saws loud into his back, three,
four inches, into his back.
Then they let him go. Not
wanting him alive, not wanting him dead.
Their knees grind over the sea
and make malice. What is love? What does love do.

Growing Darkness, Growing Light (1997) | **231**

Home

Breath entering, leaving the leaf,
the lion tense on the branch luxuriant,

the ten-foot drop to
the water-hole, the God-taste

—*that's* what lights it up,
Nature, and Art: your skin feather to feather
scale to scale to my skin

and the airy sleep, like wine . . .
two soft old children's books
with the red and blue and green crayons still warm on us.

Long Irish Summer Day

A lorry scatters
hay down the road
red as blood.

Down by Tommy Flynn's
a young man is sowing
in the ten o'clock sunset

sowing salt tears on the road
—not for the ice, we already have sand.

Sun and moon shine into our glass room,
two countries, two cities,
two glass houses:
a shotgun is hanging on the wall.

*

Dog Skin Coat
in memory of Lynda Hull

Lynda, the third, last time we talked
we talked about Mandelstam's yellow leather coat
—you told me "it was dog skin."

Ghost money, star
ledger, I'm hanging his yellow coat up here
on your coffin-door:

They'd skin a dog for a coat,
but why skin you?
Why skin a car?
Red open boat, why you?

Three nights after you died I dreamed we were thrown
out of a car. I said, "Lynda, come on, get over to the side."
You laughed, the way you'd laugh to a child, you said
"You only want to drink the gasoline."

Lynda, it wasn't dog skin.
He told his wife he wouldn't wear a coat
made out of "man's best friend."
Ghost star, is there a dog there? Any friend?

Growing Darkness, Growing Light (1997) | **233**

Fellini in Purgatory

He was shoveling sand
at the edge of the water, his heavy black glasses
glittered with rain:

"Don't you see how much like a woman I am?"
Shovel, shovel.

His throat was wrapped in water,
and the water flowered with milt.

Shoveler, are you eating the earth?
Earth eating you?

Teach me
what I have to have
to live in this country.

And he, as calm as calm, though he was dead:
"Oh,—milt,—and we're all of us milt."

Elegy for Jane Kenyon

The rooks rise off the field in a black W
and break up, black Cassiopeia breaking up
at the hour of your death. Your music is broken
and eaten among the American poets

and you are gone,
angry wolf, sad swallow,
and you are gone,
blest boat, blest water,
gone in the first hour
and gone in the second hour . . .

234 | *Light Me Down: The New & Collected Poems of Jean Valentine*

You Are Not One in a Sequence

Here
Child
who is to die
take this breast
this rattle this dress
don't listen to your friends
on the other side . . .

Child who is dead:
you are not one in a sequence.
Don't come back,
blush on your cheek,
do not push your white boat up to our dock.
Let you: stay over there, with your heaven-dog and your friends,
and we: drop back down into our intents.

Alcohol

At a memorial service
in a high school auditorium
M. in her raincoat: she

turns my hand over in hers,
she says, *At least we had July.*

Never, never, and she is gray; transparent,
fragile, made of
dusty glass,

Gilbey's Gin,
the Glass Flowers . . .

Growing Darkness, Growing Light (1997) | **235**

Where Do You Look for Me?
in memory of James L. White

They think because I am dead now
I am no longer twigs on the ground,
stones or bits of stone in the wall.
That I was just something good on a plate
for them to eat. That I have no one.

Oh my darling,
where do you look for me?

Documentary: AIDS Support Group

White paper masks over their mouths
—a piano player; an artist;
the others I don't know.

A hot light bulb, the childhood smell
of a Magic Lantern. The artist shows a slide:
closeup cracks like rivers in the leather of an armchair.

"We learned before this to read the cracks of fever,
at nine, and one, and five," the artist says.
The flat deflection of the piano player's eyes.

Poem with Words by Thornton Dial

Day by day you are being drawn
through the TV's violet needle's eye.

Luminous is the hope you have been content with.

The shaman breaks the wrist of his
countryman to get him to talk.
The film crew walk around at the edge.

A guru beams in his jazz musician's shades.

Luminous is the hope you have been content with.
—*Graveyard traveler,*
I am coming in.

A Bit of Rice

A bit of rice in a string bag:
the rice spills,
we have to sweep it up . . .
What will be left here when you die?
Not the rice
not the tea
left *somewhere* when the monk
knocked over the cup
not
not

The Night of Wally's Service, Wally Said,

"Most people will reflect back to you
however they feel about themselves,
but you have to say Hey,
don't look at me that way,

Growing Darkness, Growing Light (1997) | **237**

I'm only one day dead,
I need care.
But not Mark,
who looks at you with love.
No matter what. Like today, in church,
I was off somewhere, off Provincetown,
most people wanted me to come back,
but not Mark."

Rodney Dying

R, is sitting in a draft
—we trade places.
I see that he has a large, round hole
from the top of his head
down into his belly,
a tunnel with blood and bones around it.
He is himself,
not pretending
but completely courteous and sweet. He says,
You have to wrap your feet with paper
from now on
for this new journey.

Rodney Dying (2)

Dancing in a room full of muzak and smoke
me with my sixty years of rings
inside my fingers like trees
with this breath which is mine
and is yet not mine

238 | *Light Me Down: The New & Collected Poems of Jean Valentine*

—but my friend is dying
and there's nothing I can do
in this pure blue country.
And a voice from outside the blue window said,
"Everything is sad except what's real."

Father Lynch Returns from the Dead

There's one day a year
they can return,
if they want.
He says he won't again.
I ask what it's like—
he quotes St. Paul:
"Now hope is sweet."
Then in his own voice:
Oh well it's a great scandal,
the naked are easier to kill.

The Baby Rabbits in the Garden

—Our mother laid us there
in grass and hair.
The tunnel fell,
the farmer's boot arrived
and put us out,
too poor to stay alive.

—And now the farmer too with his large white head
backwards or forwards by a belt is led
down the black hall
hungerless to bed

Growing Darkness, Growing Light (1997) | **239**

and soon will the reader too
my listening head
be laid to bed,
the tunnel fall . . .

*

Mother and Child, Body and Soul

Child
You've boarded me over like a window or a well.

Mother
It was autumn
I couldn't hear the students
only the music coming in the window,
Se tu m'ami
If you love me

I went for a week's journey in soft ermine.
Darling, the ovals of your hair . . .
autumn leaves,
your hair the hue of rain-drenched bark, your voice:

Don't ever leave me . . .

And this child, this
window in my side,
boarded over all my life,
—how can I take the boards off, in this wind?
I will break if I bend . . .

Soul

I—as daughter—am black:
I—mother—shun her,
keep her out of everything.

The daughter says, *I'm anorexic,*
don't think I don't like the meat.   She says,

I don't want to be an animal.   *Animals*
eat other animals.

She is my soul
saying

You will never know me.
Beginning to talk.

Soul (2)

Lying in a bunk on a train
almost crushed by the woman above

strong red lipstick
big red smile

though she seems asleep. My mother is bleeding
out of the two sides of her spine,

I am putting ice on it. Freud says,
'The private is a gunbarrel.'

M. and me: two panes of glass
without even air between them.

The Mother Dreams

I'm with D. and a young woman
going into my New York apartment.
I say *It's a long time since I've been here,*
I don't know what it will look like,

—In the hall: an umbilical cord.
An aborted baby.

But it can't be mine,
I haven't been here . . .

In the next room
there are two babies
the room is flooding

the two babies are floating but soon
the water will rise.
One baby puts her finger in a socket

it catches fire
she puts it in the water.
The other is nursing from a bottle

and will drown. I take the babies
and look for help. There is none.
The medical guy leaves for home.

I saw and I did nothing.
I knew and I did nothing.

Fistula

The blood rushing under her
inside elbow skin

"Here, feel it"
rushing towards me

speeded-up water
flooding across

the fields of Ireland,
rushing away:

the silence of the mother,
the silence of the child.

Soul (3)

A man with an infant in his lap
whose throat swells up and wrinkles down
like a frog's: the man weeps,

Adapt, Adapt.
—A woman's voice:
"Always the sex-man." Desolate.

Oh my soul, *not* gone away?
When this man's starlight reaches your eye,
your eye is still
here to see . . .

Growing Darkness, Growing Light (1997) | **243**

*

Open Heart

I. EMERGENCY ROOM
The lion retreats from the cage we can see
to the cage in the back, dragging the boy who climbed
in. Bone case inside bone case.

Oh sane daylight side-
light these four,
the lion the boy myself the night.

2.
The heart was cut up into pieces
put into a Planters peanut jar
and put back on the shelf.
A bum came along
and thinking it was peanuts
he emptied it out and ate it.

3.
Eyes only

brown eyes painted with kohl
red buffalo painted on the wall

hunted, eaten
hidden in people's mouths

a face looking out from a three-foot thick
fall of bougainvillea

—your soul hides from being led
even by you

4. INTENSIVE CARE UNIT
Your shy body, turned
to silk and bone, thin blue silk
coat for what water . . .

5.
They've made a hole
in B's chest
the size of the woodworm holes
in the sideboard: threaded it
with black plastic thread:
their jump-start track to his heart.

6.
The surgeon said,
"You don't have to visit,
he won't remember it.
Ten minute visits."

Everyone here walks in a deep
open-eyed and rigid sleep.

In this deep
black unfold

we don't know what is happening to us,
no more than the dumb beasts of the field. Do they.

Growing Darkness, Growing Light (1997) | **245**

Listening

My whole life I was swimming listening
beside the daylight world like a dolphin beside a boat

—no, swallowed up, young, like Jonah,
sitting like Jonah in the red room
behind that curving smile from the other side

but kept, not spat out,
kept, for love,

not for anything I did, or had,
I had nothing but our inside-
outside smile-skin . . .
my paper and pen . . .

but I was made for this: listening:
"Lightness wouldn't last if it wasn't used up on the lyre."

*The
Cradle
of the
Real Life*

2000

* For Jane Cooper and Adrienne Rich

with affection old and true

* So long as the heaven of *Thou* is spread out over me the winds of causality cower at my heels, and the whirlpool of fate stays its course . . . No deception penetrates here; here is the cradle of the Real Life.

—Martin Buber

PART I

The Pen

The sandy road, the bright green two-inch lizard
little light on the road

the pen that writes by itself
the mist that blows by, through itself

the gourd I drink from in my sleep
that also drinks from me

—Who taught me to know instead of not to know?
And this pen   its thought

lying on the thought of the table
a bow lying across the strings

not moving
held

Elegy for Jane Kenyon (2)

Jane is big
with death, Don
sad and kind—Jane
though she's dying
is full of mind

We talk about the table
the little walnut one
how it's like
Emily Dickinson's

But Don says No
Dickinson's
was made of iron. No
said Jane
Of flesh.

Black Wolf

Suffocated in the country
a sheep in my own curtain
wolf curtain!

The black wolf nobody else saw I alone saw
trotting down the lane past our house
—Black Heart! Don't go past our house

don't get lost just when I've found you
just when life is not afraid
any more. Of me. Just when—

(I didn't *need* to hate them. You can't beat a stick.
But nobody else could see what they were like.

See it wasn't all
"on the green hill sheep
kneel and feed")—

The Cradle of the Real Life (2000) | **253**

Mother Bones

B. is dragging his mother's bones
up the stone stairs
in a bag of grass cuttings.
But you can't grow
grass from cuttings.

They lead me

They lead me to a
"lovely nurse"
"in case B. needs her"
she is   I am
sugary
melt
and disappear

I ask for a dream
about my marriage:
"Ink." Ink. Ink. Ink.

My ink-stained hand
his paint-smudged hand

gone   where
nothing joins

Your mouth "appeared to me"

Your mouth "appeared to me"
a Buddha's mouth
the size of a billboard

I thought: of course,
your mouth,
you *spoke* to me.

Then your blue finger,
of course it was your finger,
you painted with your finger

and you painted me with your finger . . .

Then appeared to me flames:
transparencements of every hand and mouth.

Mare and Newborn Foal

When you die
there are bales of hay
heaped high in space
mean while
with my tongue
I draw the black straw
out of you
mean while
with your tongue
you draw the black straw out of me.

The Cradle of the Real Life (2000) | **255**

Truth

Sharing bread
is sharing life
but truth—
you ought to go to bed at night
to hear the truth
strike
on the childhood clock
in your arms: the
cold house
a turned-over boat,
the walls
wet canvases . . .

October Premonition

October premonition

seeing my friend leave
I turn my head up, away

if she has to leave
let me not see her

my leaving mother
leaving my door open a crack
of light   crack of the depression world

Rodney Dying (3)

I vacuumed your bedroom
one gray sock
got sucked up   it was gone

sock you wore on your warm foot,
walked places in, turned,
walked back

took off your heavy shoes and socks
and swam

November

November
leaving Ireland

Sligo Bay and the two mountains
the female and the male
walking down the stairs
into the ground

—I have to leave
and I have to watch.

Labrador

Crossing a fenced-off railroad track
holes in the fence
carrying a dog

The Cradle of the Real Life (2000) | 257

my journey
I drop him
he's heavy   I can't pick him up

he puts his foot in a trap
chained to the track   a trap
yes   but that dog
won't chew his foot off
he's barking at himself   he won't let
me near.
                I left him.

1945

A year in the Pacific
watching his pilots
not come back to the ship

—they were nineteen, twenty,
they called him "Pop" . . .

We lived
for the day he came back.
The day he came back

he raged like Achilles

the day   the year   years

we flew off

one off a bridge   one into a book
one a note
into a bottle

we never came back.

—Oh my dead father
—Ah Jeanie, you're still in words . . .

Leaving

The dark black line
around the darker brown
ball of your eye

—I could only look at one eye at a time
like a horse:
white ring around the eye:

terror.
Eight years I sat on my heels in the field

waiting for you
I *wanted* to.

Running for a train

Running for a train
an older woman on my back
another old poor woman
needs help to make it too
but I can't help her too
the train has started already
the engineer
is a young woman   she
looks out the window implacably

The Cradle of the Real Life (2000) | 259

and keeps on driving
                    I knew her
I knew the old poor woman
still back at the other end of the platform
the woman slipping from me   I knew
the moon-faced boy watching by the side of the tracks

The Welsh poet

The Welsh poet
said of his mother
who "left the world"
last week
"She was never dead
in or out of it."
He shows me a beautiful Indian bird
red with yellow dots on it:
Happiness. Beauty. Art.
—That bird seems to like you.
—Yes, that bird knows
there's not much time.
The mother has a gold body now.

Radio: Poetry Reading, NPR

I heard your voice on the radio
thirty years dead
and got across the kitchen to
get next to you
breath and breath
two horses

But it wasn't you back then
I was liquid to,
it was my life:
I wanted to *be* you.
Amount to something. Be

the other
the ready stone
—prayer-rag tied to a wire fence, a branch . . .

The Tower Roof

No music
no memory
not all your art
not   not
your iron story
can fold you into the galaxy

saved by yourself
lost by yourself

your iron words
hero and chorus

This far and no farther.

For a Woman Dead at Thirty (2)

In memory
you
go through that

The Cradle of the Real Life (2000) | 261

door and go through that
door and go through that
door

cold
dark

and then the way
the sky is lightest
over eater

this world lightened

as your words
opened into their third
star-darkness

The Blind Stirring of Love

I rub my hands my cheeks
with oil   my breasts
I bathe my genitals, my feet
leaf and bark

redden my mouth to
draw down your mouth
and all along
you have been inside me
streaming
unforsakenness . . .

262 | *Light Me Down: The New & Collected Poems of Jean Valentine*

Little Map

The white pine

the deer coming closer

the ant
in my bowl
—where did she go
when I brushed her out?

The candle
—where does it go?

Our brush with each other
—two animal souls
without cave
image
or
word

The Drinker

You   breathless
drinking   drinking

making for the door
out of your life

heading out through the
chimney   the body-hole

out from the house   the skin and
bone   out from

the silence
—Love

won't take you out   death
won't take you out

nothing that's the same
will take you out

The Drinker (2)

In the doorway
your face a candle

Your face a white island
between the two currents, between the
falls of your black hair

You who drank your life greedily
hole never filled

Girl-woman who could not
whose lips could not open

Hungry ghost in the doorway

Your bones might as well have flown together and spoken:
Where is she whom my heart loves?

—Oh my darling,
where do you look for me?

Happiness

Remember our happiness?
under us   happiness
under the city
under our father' graves   happiness
under this world
under the gospel of the evangelist John:
This is the happiness he leaned his head against.

Happiness (2): The I Ching

(Alone)
"Unconcerned"
"Undaunted"

Sunset
sunrise
pines
hermit thrush

Central Park, Billie Holiday
—Misfortune. No blame

—the boat pond
rises
above the trees

: the dead don't go away
: you   "   "   "

He leaves them:

He leaves them:

No nothing's happening
you   why do you
get angry   cry
why are you leaving Me, he cries:

He turns into a moon
They turn into night bandages
He turns into strips of film
blue with another woman's blue
—loses the blue

Away from you

Away from you,
alone, I *can* come

—a leaf flickers
on the river's light skin

Together
we are two stones like one stone rolling

rolling down on the riverbed   two
light black stones

we have always been here
once we *were* one stone

—the other thing holds us
in its mouth

Child

You are in a blind
desert   child

your "too-muchness" is written
in the Torah

child   it is written
in the pit

written in black fire
on white fire

deer star
black star

third star
who sees

PART II: HER LOST BOOK

I.

Embryo

Still mermaid
inside   her
words only
half gathered

her head still floating
listening   listening
                to the Real Life

The Cradle of the Real Life (2000) | **267**

The Women's Prison

The women in the prison
are combing mannequin' heads of hair
for Beauty Care.
It's cold in there
a prison necklace of noose and lies

This bodily tool of governments
the tooth pit   the grave

In the Public Library

In the Public Library
a woman is reading a factory story
several people listening
she gets to the fire
the noise   to the locked doors   the death room
The librarian says she has to stop
it's time for him to close. He closes.

Margaret, d. 1985

At the back of the church
dressed like a bag lady, Margaret
in dark torn clothes
with her old woman smell
with the red open wound on her forehead
maggots in her wound . . .

Third floor walkup on 112th
she may have been there 85 years
the steel door open to
cat shit cat food
human shit human food
ghost dust ghost Margaret

holding tight
to her iron bed
and to empty us
of every illusion of separateness,
on her forehead
the maggots' miner's lamp . . .

At the Conference on Women in the Academy

The young scholar, her weeping finger
the anger reality
under the "social construction of reality"
under the deaf blind TV filmed
broadcast auditorium: the woman talking
in the spit-open room
under the room of what we say.

The Orphanage Landing
Goldenbridge, Dublin

We her countrypeople are deep asleep
we meet in the local
and talk in our bread-and-butter
sleep. All night the young girl waits

on the orphanage landing as Sister told her
till She comes   down the stairs
with a strap   with scalding water

In the morning the local doctor
covers the wounds up over and over
("called to the orphanage 71 times
in that year")
                        White wolves
run in: *No no this never happened.*
(White wolves in every second house are saying;
This is not happening.)

Reading the Mandelstams

Snow falling the sixth night
on the stone house full of silence
Why can't they drive you both now, tonight
up to the house, light up the house

Lines of ice
in the night window
notes

He Says to Me, In Ireland

He says to me, In Ireland
you've fallen into your destiny.
He says
the teaching and giving readings
night and day

keep him from the void. I say,
But you write about the void. I say,

All these women,
your mother,
two wives, a lover,
have died miserably,
and you have lived to write about it
your history of the world.
Or leave it out.

But I want those women's lives
rage   constraints
the poems they burned
in their chimney-throats
The History
of the World Without Words
more than your silver or your gold art.

What God Said

After she died
her son destroyed her paintings:
incinerator flames: "She wouldn't want anyone
to see this stuff." Then killed himself.

Do not fear your death, for when it arrives
I will draw my breath and your soul will come to me
like a needle to a magnet.

—"St. Mechtilde of Magdeburg" dropped down from "magnet."

The Cradle of the Real Life (2000) | **271**

*

2.

*Some of the signs suggest that you feel a leaf or
other part of a plant. A string leads from the top
of the sign to the plant.*
—Braille sign on the Miwok Trail, Muir Woods

***

She wrote a book. Lost to us
Her lost book said,
"Your search to find words
that will devour meaning
will devour you."
                    Her lost book said,
"I spent, and I earned, too:
But my money was no good there."

***

If my mother was one
and my sister was one
and my father
was not one
and my brother was not one
what was I?   I followed
the string in the dark. Alone:

***

Before the expected street into town
before the ramp Contentment
whose handrails buddle long before birth
and grew ahead of me like arms
—I stopped like a horse.

***

Something bad is happening.
No one says anything.

One by one
they get up and walk away.

They promised not to know.

Generation to generation,
bone to bone.

Poetry

You, poem
the string I followed blind
to leaf by thick green leaf
to your stem
milky
poem without words
world electric with you

The Cradle of the Real Life (2000) | **273**

The Church

"Thank you for the food," we said,
it was mashed potatoes, gravy, this
was the place the regular people came,
to go through the regular
funnel. Leaving
I saw ——— and his red
candle of "find it." My life.

***

I couldn't
he couldn't

Father I'm twenty

Whisky   marriage
children   whiskey

***

Alcohol alcohol alcohol
two children   hungry

depression's lead box
no air to breathe

Our therapist:
"You're married to a brilliant man,
you just have to accept it."

274 | *Light Me Down: The New & Collected Poems of Jean Valentine*

***

I was dark and silent.
The therapist said,
"Why don't you wear lipstick?"
To J: "Does she lie on top?"   To J:
"Don't *play her role*.
Don't give the children their baths
or feed them."

***

The soul has no   'other afternoon'
amiga gold
We   then
bandage her feet
as she steps   down and down
past where her parents pray for her
two still dark figures   kneeling in Gemini

Here there is no language

Drink   cut my wrists
drink take bad pills
into the locked ward   take good pills
can't feel   can't
or speak
or step

doctors looking down a well

The Cradle of the Real Life (2000) | 275

The Locked Ward: O.T.

Poster paints, big brushes
like my girls' kindergarten brushes:
I make a big picture, primary colors:
the social workers come like kindergarten teachers
and ask me to explain it, I so, they say,
You don't need to be here.

—Where should I be?

***

On the mental floor
I painted a picture of the children
Irreducible   altered
the MISSING children
but it was me missing.
Chewing up the mirror   the mother
was not someone else.

***

To the half-way house.
Protestant. I made
maple syrup. My friend moved in
with my husband and children.
The Methodist minister: How many men
do you have in your life.
—Sir   none.

Single Mother, 1966

No money
—the baby birds'
huge mouths
huger than themselves
—and God making
words
words

Abortion Child

I thought:
You live somewhere
deeper than the well
I live down in.
Deeper than anything from me or him.

No but it took me
time to see you, thirty earth years.

3.

To Ireland

By the Granary River
the landlord says,
"All these things—
the lambing—the commonage—

are good—yes—but they are not God."
Looking out over us
with a white and English eye.

***

Oh yes they are but
by the Granary River
we shut down seven hundred years.
My mother was in it, and hers, and hers,
my great-grandmother, hers died in the black room,
and her mother, mother to mother,
shut down and opened wrong.

Home

I left my clothes
and books
my skin
a snake
—the only one in the country!
Our sign
life   twice

***

Scarab rolling a ball of dung
across the ground
scarab hieroglyph:
to come into being:

scarab rolling with the sun
across the sky
Atlantic

***

No one's a house
for me anymore
or me for them
Home   not words but
I know it on my lips
it will come   it will melt
like ice on a stove   and I will drink it.

***

You walk across your self
as you walk across a dirt road
crossroads at dusk
and across a field   outsider
a field   and a field
steps go beside you   the sun
crossing a line   sun kind to you   sun you.

***

Under
water
look up at the dots of the sun run
along on the other side of the water line

The Cradle of the Real Life (2000) | **279**

under the white pine
the stars run along
on the other side of the sky's line   no lines

***

Snow
falling slow
filling out footprints

writing a word

changing it

night
at the window
two birches, blown together.

***

Snow falling
off the Atlantic

out towards strangeness

you
a breath on a coal

Door
in the
Mountain

2004

for Pesha & Rebecca
with love

Door in the Mountain (2004) | **283**

Annunciation

I saw my soul become flesh   breaking open
the linseed oil breaking over the paper
running down   pouring
no one to catch it   my life breaking open
no one to contain it   my
pelvis thinning out into God

*

In our child house

In our child house
our mother read to us:
England:
                there the little
English boy would love us under
neath a tree:
                not kill us:
that was white space only
like her childhood   like her
father   her sorrow

Nine

Your hand on my knee
I couldn't move

The heat felt good
I couldn't move

The shutmouth mother goes down the stairs
and drinks warm whiskey

she always goes
and drinks warm whiskey

down in the corner: Hand-
me-down:

And everything on the hair
of starting again.

The girl

spills the half-gallon of milk on the floor.
The milk is all over the floor, the table,
the chairs, the books, the dinner, the windows

—Mother and son are gone happy.
The father to work.
The sister to marriage.

The girl is still spilling
the milk-house
White negative shining
out of one life into another life.

Mother

in your white dress
your smoke
your opaque eye

you whose name
my foot
wrote

I had to die
break the rope
push through the stone fence

of you, of myself, and fly

Eighteen

Green bookbag full of poems
I leaned with my bicycle
at the black brick edge of the world

What was I, to be lost
or found?

My soul in the corner
stood
watched

*

Girl and boy
we had given each other
we wanted   breasts

bellies	hair
toenails	fingernails
hair	nipples
foreskin	foreskin
heart	

*

I gave up signing in
to the night book
little notes in time
signing our names
on the train's engine car
gray 19th century Irish men
in our gray stiff clothes

"She Sang"

Save the goat of humanity!
She started out
shot through with love books

She chose closed hearts
those she knew
would not kill her

Save her memory   her bones
dig under the house
dig near home

here at the X in the mouth of the house
the shell shocked woman   all her bones
goat bones

A Bone Standing Up

A bone standing up
she worked for words
word by word
up Mt. Fear till
she got to her name: it was
"She Sang."

The Hawthorn Robin Mends with Thorns

Talking with Mary about 1972:
like a needle
through my 25-years-
older breast my years thinner rib: 1972:

a child-life
away from my children:

"but you couldn't have been different
from the way you were"

but I *would* to have been different

Out in a sailboat

Out in a sailboat with the warden
he says so-and-so weighs 95 lbs. now
says she slept with him
because he was kind
when she was in prison

She woke up
hypnotized

A wonderful boat

She woke up
walking with the homeless
on a plank
no red schlock rope

I came to you

I came to you
Lord, because of
the fucking *reticence*
of this world
no, not the *world*, not *reticence*, oh
    Lord Come
    Lord Come
We were sad on the ground
    Lord Come
We were sad on the ground.

*

Door in the Mountain (2004) | **289**

Cousin

The erotic brown fedora on the desk:
the erotic silver watch from your father's time
balanced on its thin hinged silver lid
on the Teacher's Desk:

Once or twice, someone comes along
and you stand up in the air
and the air rises up out of the air:

One leaf
then branches
stood up in the sun consuming
—Cousin, it was happiness on earth.

The Very Bad Horse

> *The very bad horse doesn't budge until the pain penetrates*
> *to the marrow of its bones.*
> —The Buddha

My first own home
my big green "bed-sit"
in London, in 1956
double bed   green spread
sixpence coin-fed gas fire
London fog   huge little footsteps
TOK TOK TOK

I knew three people
and three more at work
I knew you

I felt around in the dark for Life
and you   I picked myself up by the hair
four stories up and dropped me

—Still I wouldn't budge.

Once

Once there was a woodcutter,
when he asked me to marry him
the woman in the grocery store said
You look like you lost your last friend.
First love!
When we broke up
it was as if the last egg in the house
got dropped on the broken floor.
    This world is everywhere! the woman said,
    You won't go unsampled!

So many secrets

So many secrets
held you in their glass

Fear
like a green glass
on the shelf

It hurt like glass
It hurt like self

Eleventh Brother

one arm still a swan's wing
The worst had happened before: love—before
I knew it was mine—
turned into a wild
swan   and few
across the rough water

Outsider   seedword
until I die
I will be open to you as an egg
speechless red

Once in the nights

Once in the nights
I raced through fast
snow to drink life
from a shoe

what I thought
was wrong with me   with you
was not wrong
                            now
gates in the dark at thy name hinge

Under the gold

Under the gold and chalk and brick, beside
the rowers on the river,

292 | *Light Me Down: The New & Collected Poems of Jean Valentine*

the black lines lived around my crayon bones.
One line.   And then my heart shut down,

even so, inside the lines.   I rode
out of the sorrowfence   blue

twine-tied gate
into the river grass . . .

The Windows

Funeral dream
"We'll put them all down in the great book of sleep."

"You may be dead but
Don't stop loving me."

In memory
"Don't hold yourself cheap,"

All the windows came to him in tears.

The chestnut tree by the North River. Its tears.

Dream   A bricklayer.   Your father.

Dream   "If you shoot someone
I will walk out on the ocean floor
and throw the gun away."

Dream   "When I am of doubt..."
Dream   "Go clear."

Door in the Mountain (2004) | **293**

Go Clear

Go clear   he said
                his high gray 19th c.
                postmortem jaw
                I loved it   its high grayness

go clear   no touch
                but words   no more
                death fear

I swam   out of the streaming ikon eyes
                who loved me: not-me: no more care
                I left the clothes
                standing there   I swam

into swarming projectless air
redemptionless
from under the earth to over the earth
air   to   not air

The Coin

While you were alive
and thought well of me
there was always a coin in my fish-mouth
off in the night
or the day lake. Now
the little coin doesn't need itself . . .

October morning

October morning—
sea lions barking
on the off-shore rock

Autumn evening—
seals' heads nosing through
the pink Pacific

I gather myself
onto my day raft, your voice
lost under me:
first other tongue

I heard my left hand

I heard my left hand love for my right hand
white through the screen door

just as through the summer elm   you
two years ago   in the bardo

moved into the room *we* once had feeling for.

In the evening

In the evening
I saw them

Door in the Mountain (2004) | 295

their little
open boats

carrying us
across the blood water

their invisible company
their invisible company

you beauty   I never
did not know

no time
no place

you beauty
little ferryman

*

We cut the new day

We cut the new day
like a key:
betrayal:

We went ahead anyway
drinking down the will of the event

On the eighth floor
something fell
alive inside the old street wall
next to the bed

I heard it fall
and fall

Occurrence of White

First thriving, then failing to thrive:
no never thriving,
from the beginning,
the ghost freighter out of Fall River,
ghost railroad car out of Chicago,
raked my skin and your skin in white silence.

How have I hurt you?

How have I hurt you?
  You saw me.

I dream I *am* you
full of fear and dread
with me in your arms
:my cloth love
holding your breath

How have I hurt you
  You saw me

I didn't see you

Door in the Mountain (2004) | **297**

Do flies remember us

Do flies remember us
We don't them
we say "fly"

say
"woman"
"man"

you   gone
through my hands
me through your hands

our footprints feeling
over us
thirstily

You drew my head

You drew my head
the back of my head
my neck stem

you made my head a charcoal skull
and even the skull
is turned away

no eyes

The little, faintly blue clay eggs

The little, faintly blue clay eggs
in the real grass nest you made and sent to me
by hand:
                It runs through my thighs, even now,
that you *thought* of it!
for a little while we thought of nothing else.
Frozen little couple in caps,
frozen beaks—

Happiness (3)

The moment you turned to me on W. 4th St.
Your gentleness to me

The hard winter grass here under my shoes
The frost

I knelt in the frost to your parents

                          The warm
light on the right hand side of your face
The light on the Buddha's eyelids

I knelt to my parents
Their suffering   How

much sleep there was in sleep   How no
suffering is Lost

Letter

The hornet holds on to the curtain, winter
sleep. Rubs her legs. Climbs the curtain.
Behind her the cedars sleep lightly,

like guests. But I am the guest.
The ghost cars climb the ghost highway. Even my hand
over the page   adds to the 'room tone': the little

constant wind. The effort of becoming. These words
are my life. The effort
of loving the un-become. To make the suffering

visible. The un-become love: What we
lost, a leaf, what we cherish, a leaf.
One leaf of grass. I'm sending you this seed-pod,

this red ribbon, my tongue,
these two red ribbons, my mouth, my other mouth,

—but the other world—blindly I guzzle
the swimming milk of *its* seed field flower—

I could never let go

my husband
my wound
my sleep

but they were surrendered from me

my books   them
pleasing you/
disappointing you

the desire for men
gazing
feeding

the cursive characters
I   my
you

in chalk across
the white-lined blackboard

surrendered from me
when I couldn't breathe so.

The Basket House

The basket house:
to shelter me
inside the night cave
the emptiness
where the other one holds me

nurses me
in the emptiness,
holds me the way
paper   made out of a tree
holds a deer.

Door in the Mountain (2004) | 301

And he holds me near:
he pulls the cord
out from me, in to him,
length over length.

The House and the World

All this anger
heart beating

unless I'd come inside
your blind window
and stay there like you

But then
the other world
was going to be given:

the cello part
carrying us the whole time

like earth   the scarred hip

tipped groin

the flying whitethorn hedge

the cup

In your eyes

In your eyes
there was a little pupil

a woman
turned to
a holy well

notes and snapshots pinned to her dress
at her feet
crutches   eyeglasses

Woman, Leaving

You waited 4 Ever

Don't listen for words here
no more than the words the grass speaks or
the mouth of the lake

Then came
an undone stitch of light
You tore it
open and flew

Trim my hoofs

Trim my hoofs!
I am thirsty for experience.

Door in the Mountain (2004) | **303**

The glass man
on the glass river says
*If only I could get
down it alone* —But
you are getting down it alone . . .

Thirsty! I drink
from my own well
the red and blue fire
around my head
this minute
vanishing   I
befriended with it

Two Poems for Matthew Shepard

But what about the blue dory—the soul

—Thief the sun   Thief the rain

Into love
the size of a silver dollar
[the soul] disappeared
to a pencil point then
nothing.
                    Left
his nails
and his hair.

The Blue Dory, the Soul

—I left the blue dory
there had been so much news
so many flashbulbs   breaking
up the dory

so many people
following their names
eating their third heavy car
their third book

I left the blue dory
on its hip   on the fence
left my soul   not "mine"
"my" clothes   off
I left the edges of "my" face
"my" hands

The Rally

The rally is about a young black man
His tongue has been cut by a razor
the tops of his ears have been cut off

My clothes   my bag
my money   my papers
                    It's
the young man

My palms
my soles
        It's
the young man

your silent invisible body here at the door
your glance

The Growing Christ of Tzintzuntzan

Come in
at the narrow door, and then
go back, but
        not yet—

Lie down,

head to my bandaged head, foot
to growing foot,
I am so tired, too,
in my glass box.

Sheep

With the winter and mud and shit roped into your wool,
Your black stick legs, blank eyes—
The farmer stumps home to his supper
And you are beyond your own bells
And my friend is in pain and there's nothing I can do,
Suffering is everywhere intense, and if
We make our own pain ourselves, who can help it? Cold selves,
Cold you, unbearable clamor and rust—

To the Bardo

I dreamed I finally got through to C on the phone
he was whispering
I couldn't make out the words

he had been in the hospital
and then in a home
M was sick too

You know how in dreams you are everyone:
awake too you are everyone:
I am listening   breathing your ashy breath

old Chinese poet:
fire:
to see the way

Rodney Dying (4)

A woman was picking up the plastic
forks and napkins in a plastic box
I was sitting on the grass floor leaning
against your knees: Under the ground
I sat down on the floor and embraced your knees.

*

Door in the Mountain

Never ran this hard through the valley
never ate so many stars

I was carrying a dead deer
tied on to my neck and shoulders

deer legs hanging in front of me
heavy on my chest

People are not wanting
to let me in

Door in the mountain
let me in

Monarch butterfly

Monarch butterfly,
dip your hand
in the wooden box
of papers on my back
and open me   Take
the hand inside the hand
I'm struggling to leave:
Let my hand play!

My old body

My old body:
a ladder of sunlight,
mercury dust floating through—

My forgivenesses,
how you have learned to love me in my sleep.

Inkwell   daybreak

Inkwell   daybreak
stairway
              stairway

Dear girls and boys,
would you go with me and tell me
back to the beginning
—so we can understand!
the journey of our lives
where we met with cruelty
but kindness, too,
and nosed up out
of the cold dark water,
and walked on our fins . . .

The path between

The path between the two twelve-foot hedges
between the fire and the window
hot on the left side   sharp on the right

something wrong   Born wrong
cleaves to itself   deflects you
Still, someone wrote something here in the dirt
and I sip at the word—

The Night Sea

The longing for touch
was what they lived out of
not mainly their bodies

For that friend
we walked   inside of the night sea
shedding our skins-

The Shirt

The shirt was going to be red:
he had to have this shirt—no other—
to stay alive, in prison.
We were setting about to cut, and sew,

but the cotton, they said, was sacred
—we had to fold it and give it back to them.
Then, even though you're so much lighter, and it was white,
you gave him yours . . .

One Foot in the Dark

People forget
Don't forget me
                You
the only white head
in the crowd of young men
live oaks
waiting to be let out of the Visiting Area.

A weed   green

A weed   green
with a black shadow village under it
and then browngray dirt   then a browngray stick
stuck on a stone
which has its own black shoah moat to the north
how hungrily life like an *o*
goes after life

Fears: Night Cabin

Snake   tick
black widow
brown recluse

—The truck last night on 79
dragging a chain

—A cloud
rounding slowly
at the window

—The wick   unlit
curled cold in the kerosene lamp.

so wild

                 so wild
I didn't notice for a long time
under your ten skins
your skull

—When life
for the fourth time touched my eyes
with mud and spit
and groaned

                —Then
I saw your and my fingerbones
outstretching in the thin blue planet water.

I have lived in your face

I have lived in your face.
Have I *been* you?
Your mother?   giving you birth

—this pain
whenever I say goodbye to thee

—up to now I always wanted it
but not this

A goldfinch in the rain

A goldfinch in the rain
a broken bird-feeder on the branch above her
its roof an inverted V   without any floor
uncradle rocking

In the Visiting Area:
rocking:
not touching

The grain of the wood

The grain of the wood
tidemarks on the beach
galaxies
fingerprints

The spark inside my ribcage
leaping at your voice
under my skin   and away in the knuckley powder . . .

The push or fly

The push or fly of the snow
here in the free woods

Your letter last night
—lost eight weeks in the prison anthrax rules—
and who knows what push/fly
at Avenal—

"... mostly freezing weather
and they don't give you anything warm to wear ..."
at Avenal,

              if I could,
I would nurse you ... as I have,
as you have me, spring weather.

I would be

I would be thick soft fleece
around your shoulders
your ill heart   at Avenal
a circle around your head
quiet against the noise, shade from the lights

Avalon

Avalon,
isle of the dead, in the west, where heroes go
after they die—
              Avenal
where do your young men go?
hot coal in no one's mouth, dying day by day
to Avenal—

Do you remember?

Do you remember? my mouth black and blue
from your starved mouth—
I didn't know anything. I didn't know I was from
the way life was before . . . your fire skin
soft as a horse's black muzzle,
soft, soft black hair
of love, white hair on your head
   —Now they have muzzled you.

That life, we couldn't stop, the sun went down,
spring snow was coming was coming

Advent Calendar

In the tiny window for December 21st,
the shortest day,

a little soldier, puppet on a stick,
or is the stick his sword? He looks quite gay.

Out my window, the woods: terrarium:
I put bread on the snow there yesterday,
but no one has come to eat it. It has frozen.
(Easy for them to follow was the child's way.)

Love they could never put you on a stick.
They could kill you in their prison
but they could never have you.

They can do anything.

Door in the Mountain (2004) | **315**

We didn't know each other

We didn't know each other,
only what we ourselves hardly knew,
though they hurt us, every breath,
the holes in our sides,
though they were invisible,
underground rivers, caves—

Touch with your finger

Touch with your finger
the left side of my chest I hunch to protect
the side that holds like a womb your walking
your walking over to us
at our plastic table in the Visiting Area
your hair cut, your chest caved in,
Your face caved in, your covered-over
silence.

Noon in the Line Outside

The pretty woman with a prisoner number, CDCP *****, written in
ballpoint on the palm of her hand. "You have to give them the
number." "You can't bring anything inside." "I'll hold your
place in the line while you go back to the car." Her clear
plastic pocketbook full of quarters for the vending machines inside.
"It has to be clear plastic." "You're allowed $30. in quarters."
I find his number, with the prison pen I write it on the palm of my hand.

Inside

Your red eye—
soap, you said
—injury?
and the darkness
around your eye
and down your cheek
—birthmark? injury?
Close close you drew me in,
Injury—

Your number is lifting off my hand

Your number is lifting off my hand
you are becoming gone

to me   but
the cut-out hurts

where you were
behind my eye

around your eye
down my cheek,

Ancient Injury—

*

Door in the Mountain (2004) | 317

The Needle North

I had a boat
lost the food
and the shoes

Hollow wrist
fill it with food
fill it with shoes

Some say we rise like dots into the sky
Walking through the show
the world begins to whirl

from this immortal coil
to that immortal coil

We whirl now into deadwood
but fire inside
                  dead wood but fire

The Passing

The shimmer
gone
out of what we know

Bells
din dan dawn
but we—down here—you little

Lord
the needle North
and move the boat

In the Burning Air

In the burning air
nothing.

But on the ground, at the edge,
a woman and her spoon,
a wooden spoon,
and her chest, the broken
bowl.

    *

She would long
to dig herself into the ground, her only
daughter's ashes
in her nose   in her mouth   her only daughter's
makeshift ashes
nothing
lying
in the hole in her chest

But her eye would still see
up   into   the ground above her, still see
the upper air

—Let her lie down now, snake in her hole, house
snake in her hold.

Little house

Little house
clay house

thousands of funeral smell
ground swell

we *knew*
the boat of right action

but the road rubbed out
—water gone!

—the dead girl gone!
(*was* she pregnant?)

dishes blew by
I searched my hollows   rubble

Burnt grass   teach me
before I forget you

into a time
when I sit and roar

over the flowers
and don't know them

Little Boat

2007

For
Eleanor Ross Taylor

Little Boat (2007) | **323**

La Chalupa, the Boat

I am twenty,
drifting in la chalupa,
the blue boat painted with roses,
white lilies—

No, not drifting, I am poling
my way into my life.   It seems
like another life:

There were the walls of the mind,
There were the cliffs of the mind,
There were the seven deaths,
and the seven bread-offerings—

Still, there was still
the little boat, the chalupa
you built once, slowly, in the yard, after school—

For her

For her,
for the tense mare and her rider
with her harness and blade
with her eyes and hooves straight ahead

with her unit   rising perfect
out of the father-ground   —"ready"—

For her,
once a foal.   For her,
born, like many a foal, born with a
wet-black line of hair down her spine—

The Artist in Prison

I will trade
what — cigarettes

for their socks
for threads

to embroider little
pictures for you

2" x 2"

I will trade

what — whole
days when I was free

     red shadow
     on the inside of my skull

for socks
for threads

for Ray Materson

In Memory

I was over at your place,
but you weren't there.
The window was covered:
a leafy gold screen,
but it was a gate, locked, double-locked,

Little Boat (2007) | **325**

and over that, thick double-velvet drapes—
And then, out of the winter blue,
there leapt from branch to branch this

monkey-armed woman.
Jumping on my back,
suffering things. She was
Addiction— I guess,
but life, too,
skating on axes on her frozen sea,
lite demanding life!
Flying life,

demanding to not-know,
demanding to know.
You. Did you ever think
you could do something useful?
You know.
Radiant?

But your touch

But your touch was everywhere, Lord
to be accomplished
though no one could see it
A great human thing was being accomplished
:   it drew every last part of him
into you
                    :   the lost sailors, diving for mines
off Korea. Every white hair,
black hair, every invisible
threshold, coarse and fine.

The Poet

for Jerry Stern

Hunger of the tongue
of the belly   the throat   even
the mike creaked
—was it hungry too? Was the lamp
wild to shine?

                       The little sounds, &
lights, & everything, alive, & veering, *fun*!
the way you tossed your head, like Johnny Cash—

Photographs at her Wake

Two curved tortoise-shell combs
in her hair
no more breathing in & out

Outside   in childhood
a glint of water
green in the limestone

Inside   in marriage
she & John in their lighted room
comb into comb

Can you feel
a hair under a page of the telephone book?
under two pages? under three?

Mattress on the floor:

my protectors blue
Mary   & Gnesh
Overcomer of Obstacles

two incense sticks
standing in the beach sand
in a yogurt cup

the old rug its dirt and fibers   its beauty
waiting   breathing

*

Night: we buried
that book of
like/dislike

Night: we read that beauty
labor of the body
Vincent   beauty from the body spun

Lord of the world!

Lord of the world!   soft
unconditional galaxies,
look at me look at me!   faraway

animal made out of dots
up in the other sky, Woman!   please you
nurse my child, please

328 | *Light Me Down: The New & Collected Poems of Jean Valentine*

nurse my other child.
Rub my hand discovered
caught in the prisoner's hand, rub
with your milk his hand.

The door is fallen down

The door is fallen down
to the house
I used to try & pry open,
in & out,
painfully,
stiff tears.

I sit underneath the cottonwoods—
Friends,
what am I meant to be doing?
Nothing. The door is fallen down
inside my open body
where all the worlds touch.

Door

Door
to the shining endless bridge
100 floors down
I can't drive this car down
No one can drive their car down
But child, they are heavy. The cars,
they will pull us down.

Little Boat (2007) | **329**

The father was a carrier

The father was a carrier
He had five buckets
How did he carry it all in those five buckets?
And the men on the ship. _They_ were all carriers,
heads and backs and shoulders — Lonely, father, little brothers,
husband, I miss you. So. Heavy-laden.

Gray

gray
"the order of the mother"
one degree Fahrenheit

News armature:

Expect sleet or snow   west coming east

> _You may not have wanted to be there_
> _It may have been because of the pain_

helicopter   on your left side
man asleep
child   on your right

Once I was girls and boys

Once I was girls and boys — now

Now who I love are the wild-
worn drifters, not of the town—

cooking their supper out by the side of the road, kisses kisses

               —And one especially, my mother's
father, lost, glare blue and shaved,

at his own work—
unknown—

on your behalf   child, window
staring for you.

The Eleventh Brother (2)

The car you were driving
flew off the bridge, it was drowning.

This was after *The Wild Swans*—
the story where even though you were her favorite

your sister couldn't finish weaving your shirt,
so when you turned back

to a man, one arm stayed a swan's wing.
The car you were driving

flew off the bridge, it was drowning.
This was after *The Wild Swans*,

your sister had finished weaving your other arm,
she dove down to give it to you

through the gray water. You couldn't
take it. You wouldn't.

"Remote Objects of Intense Devotion"

A guy smoking, in his chair
A guy in his car   intensely

in unrequited love   for Eternity
remote

objects
of intense devotion

as long as one remote glistening soul
          so long will I cry it

still forces
hotly or coldly   a child

          so long will I cry it

The first thing

The first thing this guy takes
is happiness
　　　　　　　　The faint light of the stars
　　　　　　　　In spring:　　　leaping!　lambs!

Next thing he takes
is your skin

Where it was, you grow ten more

—A lifetime learning
you could take off your skins
and just talk out of flesh, to flesh

to lamb　　　to sleep　　　to wake

That I had treated you badly

That I had treated you badly

Born and bred in The Violents, over and over
set up house with them

That I had been born half-dumb, half-blind,
my dream life more vivid than waking life, still

I remember the long gray wall
where I got out of the car. When I left them.

That I couldn't be friends
if they wouldn't be friends

That you had treated me badly

Little black coats moving away
on the flat bowl of the window, the train

Day & Night

Day & night
in the little house
breath rising, falling,
unreceived ...

What did I love most in that house? What did you? I loved
the most the early summer mornings, lying, touching, in the
farmer's square bedroom, the window lightening on the left, the
south, the home-made bed,
the beach we had swum for, old, the dog
kissing us —

All around the outside

All around the outside of the room I was given
they were lying, uncovered
in plastic rags, newspaper, rusted tin;

lying right up against the aluminum siding
of the room I'd been given,
as if it gave off warmth, the siding.

JESUS SAID,

Jesus said, Split a piece of wood, and I am there.

The Woman's Poem

An imaginary mother,
to know
human love.

Imaginary friends,
monkeys, artists, to
kiss & have fun.

An imaginary husband—
to be happy—
but he was held on an island, for life.

Imaginary
amnesty.

But the real children!

And now you say
Split a piece of wood,
and I am there.

And I am there.

Little Boat (2007) | **335**

Annunciation Poem

—my silky bed for you
in front of the fire,
a cup for your tea

I have set you a place in
side the hollow tree,
a plate for your bread—

I thought I wouldn't find you,
leaf or snow—
Rain light circles in the window, same light

circles the bread,
circles dark hair, your fontanel
—since that second you've been, been the eye of my eye.

The Poet's Poem

I thought my wearing out my shoes on poems
would please you most—
it was you, pleasing *me* most!

Longing to longing
thrown out from the stars

The Teacher's Poem

> "If you don't have red, use green."
> —Picasso

Jesus said, Fix anything—
Your granddaughter's sorrows, no.

My sorrows,
your end of life   sorrows, no.

I couldn't fix: the stovepipe,
get heat.

There was a past life I can't fix,
a future life.   " "   "

Neither the red nor the green.

Death Poem

Jesus said,
You knew me once why will you not know me
You have moved against me
Your whole earth gone
My life no use to you my death equally no

The Afterlife Poem

Jesus said,
But I *am* "alive"!

Little Boat (2007) | **337**

It's the same material,
but lighter,
summer stuff,

star-coil
Akhmatova's hair . . .

STRANGE LIGHTS

Hospital: far from home

No time alone   sun   rain
Can't talk, can't see out,
can't even see to any depth down!

What about youth?   Its car?   What about
the bride's foot?   cinnamon slipper—

Now you, Ohio
your winter fields like covers
over me—

Hospital: *At last*

> *At last I saw the broad leaf of a flower move, and*
> *underneath I saw a procession of creatures, of the color and size*
> *of green and grey grasshoppers, bearing a body laid out on a rose-*
> *leaf, which they buried with songs, and then disappeared. It was a*
> *fairy funeral.* —William Blake

Dearest, what were you doing there tonight?
Where they all understood
everything they said.

You came to make yourself a road
through the house. A *room?* you said,
is it?   It doesn't measure out.

A poem?   You cut it into pieces,
slept under it.

Time—you bore it on a green leaf
under the ground.

Hospital: strange lights

I needed a friend but
I was in the other room
—not just the other room,
another frame
dragging   blue
or brighter blue: strange lights:

The doctor singing from *The Song of Songs*
'in the secret places of the stairs'

Us standing there   in the past
as we were
in life
you turning and turning my coat buttons

Hospital: It was euphoria

It was euphoria
little veins of it sent

burst to the brain
three little fireworks
white on the gray MRI

it was euphoria

when you stove my boat
& brought me over
listing in the racing foam—

Hospital: Scraps

Scraps of hard feelings
left on the floor
winter material

But out the window
sun on the snow
Dressmaker's pins
—somebody's soul
a feminine glint in the trees

A BOWL OF MILK

The Look

Pain took me, but
not woke me— no,
years later, your
look
woke me:
each shade & light:

to earth-love then
I came,
the first
beach grasses.

I wanted to be sure to reach you

—But to go away!
And I wanted to be sure to reach you!

And the charge still in us   ankle waist & wrist
& eyes   —Not see you!

Or you to reach me, so
with our townspeople at last we could rest.

But to you now I offer — forgive me, River —
what I could never then, give over.

When she told me

When she told me over the telephone you died
I lay down and cried, "Don't you stop loving me."

In the West Side Market, I heard your voice
from the ceiling say out loud to me, I love you.

In the park, to a chestnut tree,
to the light through hundreds of leaves, I said, I love you.

It *was* you.   And it was my life, run, to what,
—you closer than touch.

This Side

The grave window-eyes across the street
look in, eyes open, half-open,
or gone asleep.   Madonna
Lord.   I wait,
antenna out at an angle,
wrapped with aluminum foil, the radio
turned this way or that—or the aerial
snaps right off & I carry it with me,
caduceus.

                    And I left
a bowl of milk outside the threshold the night
the souls of the dead return, & in the morning
licked it where he licked.

His White Jade Eggs

Is the train I'm on, moving?   or is it
the train next to this one?

It's floaters
                drifting off & up & out of sight,
the whole November city, jazz, the white eggs,

No more those oval in-breaths & out-breaths of his—

I was lying there

I was lying there, half-alive
in a wooden room at a Russian country place.
You sat by me quietly.   It's true you left
sometimes, but came back, sat by me
kindly   quietly.
Woodsman, would you go back to the little-
light-wrapped trees
and turn them on again?
The hide of the deer shivered
The summer wind riffled through my hair.
                                        You are on
a long, patient, summer visit from death.
I am forgiven.   Forgiving.   To your place
the next to be born.

Little Boat (2007) | **343**

The Harrowing

The worn hands
spines   feet
           Even he
whose blank hand I held on to
for dear life
           phantom limb

On your sidewalk
walking past your café

the piano was being tuned, hard,
trying it, one note at a time

trying, walking outside of time
—was that the night—   & space

Blessed are those
who break off from separateness

theirs is wild
heaven.

344 | *Light Me Down: The New & Collected Poems of Jean Valentine*

FROM THE QUESTIONS
OF BHANU KAPIL

Where did you come from/how did you arrive?

From Tipperary.   In swaddling clothes.

Slowly I followed for the far opening
in the long cloth tunnel

This is what birth was like, I thought—
trying to follow the body

up its stem to the air—
                                        I couldn't
find my way out.   Only throw myself out

against the restraining blankets, cold, wet
swaths of home.

What is the shape of your body?

Staunch meadows for the children
reservoir

Reservoir
your thin ghost-body

Whatever kind of eyes
you have now, lend to me—

What do you remember about the earth?

All night long I listened to the coal train,
I whirled, I davened,
I danced, I skipped like the hills,
and I was satisfied.
All night long I lay on my bed,
my throat sang, and I was satisfied.

What are the consequences of silence?

A quilt of mothers and children:
your name embroidered with red thread
in cursive on a white square
against the gray field of the quilt, your
name along one side   your mother's name
—Was she eighteen?   along another side beside
another mother & child of 1922:

Your name & your mother's name, the surname
was made up, an anagram, you told me, years later:
your mother & father
could not marry.   The night I saw the quilt
on my uncle's bed where I slept the night he died,
it was my grandmother's quilt from a church sale,
I was twenty, your student.

I was going to tell you about it, your name, but the air
was too thin, I couldn't.   I wrote you about it,
but you never answered or spoke about it;
two years later, we were in love, and still
never talked about it: not about the quilt, not about
our lips that never touched—

How will you /have you' prepare(d) for your death?

quiet   ready
the wires inside the walls

and when no wires
and when no walls

—with you it wasn't flesh & blood, it was under:
I know you brokenheart before this world,
and I know you after.

MARIA GRAVIDA,
MARY EXPECTANT

Maria Gravida

Then the gold mother began her touching me
With her long brown face & hands
She tickled me & told me I was beautiful
She held me in the ikon & we gazed

We had a pretty goldfinch   death   salvation
Love was strong as death   Peacocks walked by
Blue immortality   Finches played in black branches
Souls around the cross   It was death in life

Our gold earth gravida
Not a casket but a darkroom for our love
The herma wrought of silver, gilded in fire
Gold mother around me inside me gravida

Little Boat (2007) | **347**

Eye of water

I have nay ben nn
To keep nn safe
I cannot keep them safe

If nn tway
If nn thee

Keep them
Eye of water

Moose and calf

Moose and calf eat the shoots of the willow trees
along the Alaska highway
looking for you

thirsting after don't know
before I can't remember you any more
Call to me!   friend

whose heart in your side is broken in two
just by a chance comma of time;
still, within the wound in your side

is *a place*
inviting fair—large enough (I saw)
to offer refuge for all.

To my soul (2)

Will I miss you
uncanny other
in the next life?

And you & I, my other, leave
the body, not leave the earth?

And you, a child in a field,
and I, a child on a train, go by, go by,

And what we had
give way like coffee grains
brushed across paper . . .

The Rose

a labyrinth,
as if at its center,
god would be there—
but at the center, only rose,
where rose came from,
where rose grows—
& us, inside of the lips & lips:
the likenesses, the eyes, & the hair,
we are born of,
fed by, & marry with,
only flesh itself, only its passage
—out of where?   to where?

Then god the mother said to Jim, in a dream,
Never mind you, Jim,
come rest again on the country porch of my knees.

Break the Glass

2010

for Kate and Max Greenstreet

a pencil

for a wing-bone

Lorine Niedecker

I

In prison

In prison
without being accused

or reach your family
or have a family   You have

conscience
heart trouble

asthma
manic-depressive

(we lost the baby)
no meds

no one
no window

black water
nail-scratched walls

your pure face turned away
embarrassed

you
who the earth was for.

The whitewashed walls

The whitewashed walls, the chair
Were we nursed by the same wet-nurse?

The cups of tea undrunk
The crumb of tobacco on your lip

The poems in our speckled notebooks
where we warmed our hands

over the quick fire

Long before the woodstove's wood and coal
shifted and settled and warmed us

Even months before
Even from miles away

The Leopard

Like a leopard on a shield, the space leopard
lay down beside the basket,
and slowly I threw all the papers in.
I was glad to throw them in.

Every coldness ever breathed
had left its trace elements inside me;
the oldest mother god's most silent love
had left its trace: her
cave paintings black and gold
& red in the caves of my body.

In the end,
I laid them all down there at the leopard's feet,
I was glad to lay them down.

Even all night long

Even all night long while
the night train

pulls me on in my dream
like a needle

Even then, down in my bed
my hand across the sheet

anyone's hand
my face anyone's face

are held
and kissed

the water
the child

the friend
unlost.

I was working

I was working on cleaning up a house
before I left it.

The longest work every year was Clean the house
before we moved.

The mother as a child was always moving,
who knows why.

I, said the fly.
With my little eye.

If I clean up this house here long enough,
I can leave it.

But leave the eye next to where I
put my house, this way, that way—

"As with rosy steps the morn"
in memory of Lorraine Hunt Lieberson

Everyone
on the other side of the earth
standing upside down, listening,
Everyone on the reverse of the picture
on the other side of the measuring eye

The five notes, slowly, over & over,
and with some light intent,
And the whole air,
no edge, no center,

And the light so thin, so fast—

*

Don't listen to the words—
they're only little shapes for what you're saying,
they're only cups if you're thirsty, you aren't thirsty.

Dear Family,

> "[the chrysalises] came out with their wings
> packed down... like crumpled letters... Some
> did not get quite free..."
> Rebecca Solnit, *A Field Guide to Getting Lost*

November 1862. Dear Family,

Lying here tonight, looking into the fire, waiting for fire,
I was seeing our fire at home, in my mind's eve:
Mother, the little girls—
but then gunfire— we took up our guns
I'd have gone forward, but
then went the right eye of my body,

Mother,

don't read this yet,
my thoughts are still packed down
like crumpled letters, and some of us
will not get quite free—

356 | *Light Me Down: The New & Collected Poems of Jean Valentine*

Canoe

Listen to the crescent
Listen to
the thin old house

Black Elk
smoking with us

pulling to us
up to the late dock
the canoe

Not enough bark
It was stretched till it broke
Patched, pale colors

An old horse, almost completely blind

A map
to *the end of this world or cycle*

The Japanese garden

The Japanese garden
is tilting quietly uphill

—eleven wet green stones,
bamboo, and ferns—

It might be under water,
the birds be fish, colored in.   And you,

masked reader: the glance
of your underwater lamp,

your blackwater embrace—
not bought or sold.

Ghost Elephants

In the elephant field
tall green ghost elephants
with your cargo of summer leaves

at night I heard you breathing at the window

Don't you ever think I'm not crying
since you're away from me
Don't ever think I went free

At first the goodbye had a lilt to it—
maybe just a couple of months-
but it was a beheading.

Ghost elephant,
reach down,
cross me over—

On a Passenger Ferry

in memory of Grace Paley

The deck is big, and crowded. In one corner,
an old woman, sick, on chemo, not in pain, is
writing in an elementary school notebook.
Nobody else saw her, but I saw her.
I had seen her before. Her round, kind face,
smiling and still as a photograph
outside a window—

Then Abraham

Then an old man came down out of the thicket,
with an axe on his shoulder, and with him

two people made out of light
—one a blameless son,

the other like a Vermeer girl,
on their way back down with the old man.

Still, all the history of the world
happens at once: In the rain, a young man

holds out a blue cloth
to caress her head

at the landing-pier
of the new bride.

You can't get beauty. (Still,
in its longing it flies to you.)

Traveler

A matchbox painted and figured
with five gardeners
and thirty-seven flowers, red and blue,
a pretty garden.
One little fellow stands off.
Anybody can see
love is all around him,
like the blue air. Most
dear in the Double Realm
of music, he is a Traveler.
He stands off, alone.
When somebody dies, as is the custom,
he burns the place down.

Coyote

Walking last night in the drought-country dark
she heard wolves howl. No,
coyotes.

Sexual love
coyotes crying
breathing close

This morning it was on the radio
it's turning a little cooler, she is turning

She has given her purse of money
away, it's time
to turn back into Coyote

My, my Coyote in the doorway

Hawkins Stable

It was years before you could climb
back up over the fallen stalls, and knock at
the family's old door

                  —they were gone,
you could just look in from the road.
Field after field.
Your eyes looked two ways at once.

                    Under the fields,
the dense tongue of the cow—
and the horses' eyes—

and the water from the hand-pump in the sink,
racing like horses.

I I

Who watches
for Dr. Paul Farmer

Who watches
on a moon-surface hillside
the soon-dead children's rubber ball
circle in an oval
sunstruck orbit,
from hand to hand...
Cange,
Haiti,
Earth

Time is matter here

Time *is* matter here
The freight train
I saw in the morning
still in the evening
inching across the flatlands
word after slow word
too many to count

And you are matter—
your eyes, your long legs,
slow breath sometimes catching
in your sleep, your head
resting against the bus window,
tired horse,
tired rider

Earth and the Librarian

At the library
she passed a tray with little
books of baked earth on it—

—Take one,
and eat it;
It is sweet,
and it is given for you.

—Who lives in me?
said Earth—

Her car

Her car had hit another car.
The other driver's insurance person called.

It was all going well,
a matter of time.

She lost her tongue. It was her taste
for life, for herself, for others.

She found her tongue on the floor
and paper-clipped it to

the kitchen calendar. This was back in the day
of Separation. Permanence.

The World inside This One

> There is another world
> but it is inside this one
> —Éluard

Steamer trunks
standing on end
standing open
like big books

The world inside of that one
mass graves
like in this one

Inside of that world
someone painting
animal-souls

Inside the dark
huge sounds

Poet

I'm standing there
behind your grandparents, proud,
saying goodbye:

you with your three dresses,
your prettiness,
going up to the city—and beside you
the devoted, tall shadowy monk.
(Two were seen leaving.)

(Two were seen leaving.)

And inside them   deep space
And deepspace loves them

moving slowly its thumb
across to the speck of gold there
there on her lip

but not hunger

or hunger not granted

The treeless hill

The treeless hill that gave holes
in its dirt cliff to the swallows
in the long wet light of June, the open
cliff by the road that gave
them nests, your cold wet sweater,
sweater you were born in, softer then,
like any swallow

The just-born rabbits

The just-born rabbits in the garden
huddled blind, translucent, hardly here

I called John (a farmer),
and asked him what to do:

*Put your boot on them. Now you've been there,
the mother will never come back.*

—life from whom
death also springeth green
—thy leave to sleep

The valley

The valley
edge by edge
bare field by field
I walked through it through you

rain by rain
cold by cold
root absence
and the purposeful cold

Eye opened
slow
but what is slow

On the bus

the ghost-bus travels along beside us
and the reading-light,
a straight-faced little moon

And you cloud, ragged, legless rabbit
with your long nose
and your enormous eye

Tell me
What is the name for a non-endstopped line?
Who was it M. looked like?

Was it Kafka?   Kafka,
is that your enormous eye?
Ecstatic eye,
still see us.   your same clay

The branches

The branches looked first like tepees,
but there was no emptiness.

Like piles of leaves waiting for fire:
at the foot of the wisewoman trees,
at the foot of the broken General.

Next to the tree of the veteran
girl who died this summer.   slow red
cloth

Red cloth

Red cloth
I lie on the ground
otherwise nothing could hold

I put my hand on the ground
the membrane is gone
and nothing does hold

your place in the ground
is all of it
and it is breathing

Break the Glass (2010) | **367**

I I I

Don't silence yourself, *No te calles*

He took some words from the bowl
and placed them on the table
No te calles

I took some too
placed them near to his words
      Martín Ramírez

After,   slowly, slowly
from childhood
towards him   followed my footsteps

circling sometimes
sometimes falling.   in a quite practical way
to sleep   to speak

Eurydice who guides

Eurydice who guides   Orpheus who guides
who first has to return to death
the one who sings
the one who opens first
of all the animals his
mouth to her song
her thirst his thirst
the ones who nurse each other

Don't be afraid the blackened saucepan said
I met them in the country by a well

and once I drank from them
I never thirst

If a Person Visits Someone in a Dream, in Some Cultures the Dreamer Thanks Them
          in memory of Reginald Shepherd

Dear Reginald,
It is morning.
I sit at a table
writing a letter
with a needle and thread.

*

I pricked my finger   A pelican
out of her migratory path,
even her language family—
whose child is gone
yet she absently pecks at her breast.

*

I write on the bedspread
I am making for you there
May you breathe deeply and easily.
If a person visits someone in a dream,
in some cultures the dreamer thanks them in the morning
for visiting their dream.

*

I call it dream
not that I am drawn to that which withdraws
but to him *pearled, asleep*, who never withdraws.

*

At a hotel in another star. The rooms were cold and
damp, we were both at the desk at midnight asking if
they had any heaters. They had one heater. You are
ill, please you take it. Thank you for visiting my dream.

*

Can you breathe all right?
Break the glass   shout
break the glass   force the room
break the thread   Open
the music behind the glass.

*

Remember that blue vine?   Grown
                        alongside the gate

fourteenth century
                        Venus close as the moon

the bowl of the skull   turning here
                                lifting that

I dropped a plate

I dropped a plate and broke it
it came from a set

I keep the scraped-down leak marks from the rain
on the wall from two years ago
layers blue and tan

370 | *Light Me Down: The New & Collected Poems of Jean Valentine*

Page 7

Page 8

The broken, the underneath,
the backwards:

On the radio, Merce said, *Do it backwards,*
Jump first, then run,
even if it was just with his arms, when he got old,
even if some people hated it

Desert Prison

If every present is possible,
how can we have eyes to see?

The teacher and I, the guest, both free, class over,
just walking down the corridor, out to the gate

The teacher and I, looking wildly
how to mend
the man's head that the other man had stabbed—

Where to wash
your head   that they had stabbed

You kneeling, by the door,
trying to get out of the corridor—

You ask,

Could we have coffee? —No, my truth,
I'm still on this side.
             I saw you last night, again,

at the bar on 57th,
O faceless dancer,
and I put down my mask

I wanted you to touch me
You stood there neither man nor woman,
beautiful edge   by the water

The Young Mother

Milk called out of the breast
to the just-born mouth

Inside the earth
earth came

All membrane
no sound

—orgasm—god—
be my unshareable secret?   unreceived?

I'm sad, Warden
Are you sad

All you people looking out from the stern
of the white ship *Withholding*

—I'll take my babies
and swim

I thought It's time

I thought It's time to go into the forest with a bowl.

Maya said, *It's all one thing,*
student, householder, forest.

The blue man said,
You are the forest and the bowl

—as he made a trail of tobacco, or cornmeal,
back to the foot of my chair.

Jack said,
You don't need
a bowl. Putting his cupped hands together
in front of him on Eighth Street

—the trees walking toward us
hands cupped in the light of Eighth Street.

On the CD, in the rainstorm
in memory of Michal Kunz

On the CD, in the rainstorm
the healer whispers what he hears from his guides.
His whispers are a quiet-stepping rainstorm
stepping across the room.

                    Michal
—I hope you don't mind my saying this—
sits down with us and looks up into the rain.
They say
he will write
if not his poems
other poems.

Old love, I want to phone you

I miss another body in this life.   But miss
you, turned-away?
Can I miss not-love? The centuries say
Sure possible, all the languages say, all the
bodies, the trees. Ice storms.
                    In her room
a student cuts angular lines
into her arm.
The blue man says, *Don't cut, they're saying* (he listens, whispers,
then he talks) they're saying   *For the present*
A body by herself cán be in love on earth.

Diana

The tab on the tea bag said
"Love what is ahead
by loving what has come before."
But what came before was no dream
you wake from, it was human sacrifice:
Diana was herself, and Actaeon, who saw her naked,
and the stag he was turned into

(who was God)
and the blind dogs
and the death of God
"for the sin of seeing."   God
still childbearing, naked, seeing.
Do we get another life?   *Oh yes.*
Maybe not in this place.   Maybe in different forms.

The older man among us

The older man among us looked right through me.   Lost.
Without expression.   Long look.   Who were you?
I had a glass of water in my hand.
Are you my grandfather?   Would you like to drink?
I wished I was a horse, and I could lay
my head over your neck.

He Disappeared into Complete Silence

The wild ladders of longing
no longer pieces of wild wood, sawed off
and fitted to each other,
no longer stored in a closed-off room
with one blank window

But called back, through
the closed-off wooden ceiling, to his
speech returned.

I am fain a page in the court of space

I have pulled the elements in no order
in around me, like a blanket:
elephant blanket.
It will harden when I take it off.
my skin, when I
leave you on the ground and walk away.

A page   air
a pen   water
books   earth
friends   fire

I V

Lucy
for Sister Leslie, C.H.S.

Lucy, whose skeleton is approximately 3.2 million years
old, whose genus and species are "*Australopithecus
afarensis*, or 'southern ape of Afar,' after the region of
Ethiopia where the bones were found," was discovered in
1974, at Hadar in northern Ethiopia. "The Ethiopian
people refer to her as 'Dinkenesh,' an Amharic language
term meaning 'You are beautiful.'"

Lucy
your secret book
that you leaned over and wrote just in the dirt—
Not having to have an ending
Not having to last

376 | *Light Me Down: The New & Collected Poems of Jean Valentine*

...in thy book all my members
were written, which in continuance
were fashioned, when as yet there
was none of them.
>   —PSALM 139:16

Two hands
were all you owned

for food
for love

Now you own none, Lucy
nor no words

only
breath marks

breath marks
only

nor no words
Or what *do* you do now Lucy

for love?
Your eyeholes.

Lucy
my saxifrage that splits the rocks
wildgood
mother

you fill my center-hole
with bliss
No one is so tender in her scream
Wants me so much
Not just, but brings me to be   Is
when I am close to death
and close to life

The spider
in her web three days
dead on the window Lucy

In the electricity of love, its lightning strike
or in its quiet hum in the thighs
like this little icebox here
not knowing any better
or in the dumb hum of the heater going on
little stirs in the room-tone
I rush outdoors into the air you are
Lucy
and you rush out to receive me
At last there you are
who I always *knew* was there
but almost died not
meeting
          when my scraped-out child died Lucy
you hold her, all the time.

Lucy
when the dark bodies
dropped out of the towers

When Ruth died
and Grace
and Helen Ruth

And Iraq
and Iraq

And Nikolay

Lucy, when Jane in her last clothes
goes across   with Chekhov
you are the ferryman, the monk
Ieronim
who throws your weight on the rope.

I wash my plate and spoon
as carefully as a priest.
Did you have a cup, Lucy?
O God who transcends time,
let Lucy have a cup.
You bodhisattva here-
with-us. You wanted to come back!
I'm afraid
and can't pay attention
to it   I'm
wild with heat and cold
and my head hurts:
The nine wild turkeys come up calmly to the porch
to see you, Lucy

Break the Glass (2010) | **379**

My Work of Art
for Lucy

It's a piece of brown wrapping paper
taped to the wall   over the table
in this beautiful room with no pictures
First, written across the top:
"It was as if she was standing
across the road
waiting to see if anyone
wanted to get to know her."

Then taped under that:

Du, der du weißt, und dessen weites Wissen

>*You who know, and whose vast knowing
>is born of poverty, abundance of poverty—*
>
>*make it so the poor are no longer
>despised and thrown away.*
>
>*Look at them standing about
>like wildflowers, which have nowhere else to grow.*

Then a blue panther, a twenty-six-cent stamp
from Florida, for postcards

Then a catalpa leaf curving
from its huge curving stem, the leaf

a little broken in its passing
from the West down to the East

and the note: I found this leaf
on my way to the Post Office.

Then Lucy you: hominid? sapiens?
sapere, to taste, be wise

Your skeleton
standing about, like a wildflower...

Lucy, what you want,
that I will do.
To hear you now.
Your poem. (But you need nothing.)

The deer and the wild turkeys
that draw close now to hear you.
My life is for.
In its language.
Your voice.

I can't tell cold from heat.
Anxiety
dust.
Death, no
not even dust.

Your Picture

Brown museum hair, brushed the way they brush it there,
brow lit from inside,
intelligent eyebrows,
a slightly wrinkly nose, a little flat—
brown woman, I want your nose, your
cheekbones of light—I was brown, I got white—

Break the Glass (2010) | **381**

Your large and friendly mouth, half-open
in a half-smile,
like the Dalai Lama once, in a procession,
his smile "What am I doing here?"

But Lucy
your eyes.

So I gave all I had to the poor, standing about
like wildflowers.

Lucy,
the spider moved, last night,
and again, this morning...

I wonder Do you sleep and wake
where you are now? Do spiders
hibernate? Do they lay eggs
in webs on windowpanes?

                              You must know
everything.

Enter the sweet Why
Don't entreat it
or question why
whistle why
whisper why
was sweetness done to you
done unto you
What I wanted most   the mother

382 | Light Me Down: The New & Collected Poems of Jean Valentine

has come to me
Will she stay in my ear? Lucy
Is it you?
Still all night long my
Lucy I entreat you
I will not let thee go except thou bless me.

Outsider Art

Martín Ramírez,
be with me!
"It looks just like a vagina,"
a bystander said. Yes
it is a vagina, with trains, and tunnels,
and like in the great cathedrals,
a clitoris, a starry one,
and a womb, jaunty Martín being born, Lucy
did you hear animal-woman
screams in the night?
Were you afraid?
Was it you last night
your scream over and over
as you give birth?

How did you pray, Lucy?
You *were* prayer.
Your hands and toes.
When writing came back to me
I prayed with lipstick
on the windshield
as I drove.

Newton made up with the world,
he had already turned himself
into gold, he was already there.

Skeleton Woman,
in   down
over   around

Bless:
from the Old English *blētsian*.
Its root is *blood*.

My head is at your window, Lucy, at your glass,

But we offer nothing but money now,
we beam it to each other near and far,

But you are my skeleton mother,
I bring you
coffee in your cemetery bed.

This morning I miss most of all you, Martín,
and her who when you were born
looked and blessed your beauty.
Lucy, when you are with me
I feel the atoms
racing everywhere
in this old oak table,
in the eight-pointed double-star spider,
and in the starry rippling all around us.

Skeleton Woman, Guardian, Death Woman, Lucy,
Here, a picnic, corn bread, here, an orange
with Martín and me at the lip of the Earth Surface World.

Shirt in Heaven

2015

for Emily Wilson
2002-2013
in loving memory

LUNA MOTH

Luna Moth

Luna moth
at the black window

I hold you in my signal-memory
but I can't get back to how to talk to you,
silent as the black window.

Silent as your body
little book
on which
I in my hunger wrote.

A Child's Drawing, 1941

A woman ladder leans
with her two-year-old boy in her arms.
Her arms & legs & hands & feet
are thin as crayons.

The man ladder
is holding his glass of bourbon,
he is coming out of the child's drawing
in his old open pajamas—

he's in the war. The sky
is blackest crayon-canyon.
When does he leave again? When he leaves,
I leave.   I like that river the sky.

1943: The Vision

I saw it when I was nine
alone.   looking into a shed

a human head.   cut in two.   lengthwise
in profile, lifelike, in a museum-size
glass jar, on a shelf.

I knew what it meant:
You must put the head back together again.

How could I put the head back together again?
But I promised. Everyone promised: dark eyes
to dark eyes.

Forest, Stars

Now the stars didn't show:
It was after the forest fire,

after her friend had lost his thinking
in the war—   after

he had come upon a silence:
blood   saliva   semen   her

Shirt in Heaven (2015) | **389**

Her last year

Rest your mouth.
Rest your music.
Rest your walking around.   Sit down.
Drink.   Eat.

With my eyes, I see you eat stones.
I see you eat bones.
You eat mud. You eat the light.

I don't recognize anything.

Not a sign, a cut, a knife, a dark wood, a net.

I recognize everything.
The sign, the cut, the knife,
the dark wood, the net.

for Marina Tsvetaeva

God of rooms

God of rooms, of this room made of taken-away
papers and books, of removal, this single
room made of taken-away
empty now, god of empty rooms, god of
one unable to speak, god of turned-over boats
in the wind (god of boat and mouth and ear)

listen to someone, be of-you
needful to someone

for Paul Celan

Hold the finch

Hold the finch who flew into the window
till he can fly. But the window
flies into his face, over & over.

*

Send warm clothes,
send money.

Not knowing the last part
when or how would you die
—in want of

warm clothes, money,
for the last part

(no longer granted your friend)

*

She took her pocketbook,
her clothes, set out,
no company, no deeds,
a hoard of words.

*

Lie down, living human thought,
let your anxious glance like a house cat's glance
ask in its speechless rising and setting,
Do I concern you? Am I there?

for Osip & Nadezhda Mandelstam

1945

The winter trees offer no shade no shelter.
They offer wood to the family of wood.

He comes in at the kitchen door, waving like a pistol
a living branch in his hand, he shouts
"Man your battle stations!"

Our mother turns to the kitchen curtains.
He shakes the branch, a house-size Big Dipper

points north over the yard:
Can it help? How about

the old dog, thumping her tail. Whose dog is she?
How about the old furnace, breathing.

Breathing the

world: a flier, a diver,
kitchen curtains, veterans, God, listen kindness,
we're in this thing like leaves.

For love,

you leapt sometimes
you walked away sometimes

that time on the phone you
couldn't get your breath
I leapt but couldn't get to you

I caught the brow that bid the dead
I caught the bough that hid

I'm, you know, still here,
tulip, resin, temporary—

Shirt in Heaven

Come upon a snapshot
of secret you, smiling like FDR, leaning on your crutches—

come upon letters I thought I'd burned—

I suppose you've got a place with lots of stairs.

I'm at the end of something, you're at the beginning.

I'd be rich, I'd get you an elevator:
a rare old smoky wood one.

I was at the beginning, so I was the oldest:
a looking-away door that opens at your touch.

—dearest, they told me a surgeon sat down
in the hospital morgue, next to your body, & cried
He yelled at the aide to get out.

His two sons had been your students
—me too, little-knowing—

there's nothing when

there's nothing when you're young and clare
but love and nowhere for it
for it to go but your
sweet open eye to the wounded
eye of the beloved
Then the bony aloneness
forty years &
forty years
and then   your eye again
& now we talketh all day long
& every night I keep my window
at your window   Yet my arms
get pulled out into   incomprehensible wind   Yet
you sweetly ask
in the silk wind
Will I come

Peace to bad waters

driftwood   seaweed
your sleeping arms, earthless
profile, drift,

Sleep, finished
here, bad waters, peace,
sadness drawn
across your mouth, peace

Bardo

You were picking through a trash bag,
taller than you.
Taking out anything worth something.

Our eyes met. I thought
What keeps us here? Two-legged?
You looked right through me.

My teacher says, just say to yourself,
Something will happen.
Something happen.

I could take off my clothes
and leave them on the ground.
I could walk off into the snow

out of human sight, out of

all the northern evening's gold brocade

Shirt in Heaven (2015) | **395**

W. 13th Street

I saw a table on the sidewalk
after snow   Candles,
wineglasses, a penciled note
Remember that I love you

Tall snow and the huddled cars.
The table like a car opening down.
I went down through, & I saw
a country picnic was prepared for you

who scree the dark canyon incognito
thin line of black hair you were born with, down your spine.

Open

I lay down under language
it left me and I slept

—You, the Comforter, came into the room
I moved my head—

my blood, my mouth
all buttoned away—

Makers of houses, books, clothes-
makers, goodbye—

A leaf, a shadow-hand

A leaf, a shadow-hand
blows over my head
from outside time
now & then
this time of year, September

—this happens—
—it's well known—
a soul locked away inside
not knowing anyone,
walking around, but inside:

I was like this once,
and you, whose shadow-hand
(kindness) just now blew over my head, again,
you said, "Don't ever think you're a monster."

You rope that pulls them where they do not go

horse running sideways
on only water

no school   no teacher   fire
made out of fire
poison houses

children in a rough line
holding onto a rope

a man with a cell phone pulling the rope
the reception breaking up

*

The man *had* to leave the books behind
Leave night behind   I know you don't use words there

sleepwalking a word-scrap   Day-walking my Redeem'

I'm lifting something very light   a blanket
Outside the window you're lifting something very heavy

Pat the rope then
chew the rope apart

I know you don't have teeth there
I know you don't have hands there

The helicopter,

The helicopter,
a sort of controlled silver leaf
dropped lightly into the clearing.
The searchlights swung, the little girl,
the little girl was crying, her mother, a girl herself,
was giving birth, the forest dropped birdseeds of milk.
Then the helicopter lifted away,
the mother rested.

                Like him who came to us empty-handed,
who came, it seemed, with nothing,
Joseph Cornell—   making
a shoebox universe to put it all in.

When I lost my courage

When I lost my courage and my thought
God still sat sewing by the window.
I threw myself to everywhere—
the harbors, everywhere
the poets & painters were.

The dancers—
misunderstandings
higher, deeper, colder—
but beauty—
but the lovers' curtained Dutch beds
over & over
sewn together & torn again—

His hand takes

His hand takes after me with a knife.
His blanked-out eye looks out   sharp
and does not like what it sees.   "Cunt."

        After everything there,
the tall Marys—most dearest cunts—
and little Keats rested in with me,
under the bridge of the lamplight—

Until day came, and the day driver.

Shirt in Heaven (2015) | **399**

Bury your money

Now, there: there's the money.

Great captivities tap
in our sleep.

But we made a promise   God and us
to meet in another life
when we both could want it.
If only one of us wanted, that
wouldn't be enough.
We made a promise to be naked
—though great famines bury the ear and the mouth,
though captivities cut parts away, or swell, or sap them,
we made a promise to be naked, John Cage said
Music is continuous; only listening is intermittent.

Poem with endwords by Reginald Shepherd

I saw it—there's
the bright snow—it's never
going to be enough
for this intimate world
—never enough for
the third strange angel, you.

She will be

She will be
a standing gong
struck from inside
that will go on sounding out
from her own stomach, no, *the*
little thumb-like object in her chest

it's making its sound
in her room
or in a desert someplace   sound-waves   my conscience
My conscience *knows*
its hurt   Most
strange & lucent thumb, told it

for Alice Notley

F R I E N D

[The ship] is slowly giving up her sentient life, I cannot write about it.

Shackleton, diary

Next to where their ship went down
they pitched their linen tents.

You, mountain-climbing,
mountain-climbing,
wearing your dead father's flight jacket—

My scalp is alive,
love touched it. My eyes are open water. Yours too.

Sitting in the dark Baltimore bar
drinking Coke
with you with your inoperable cancer
with your meds

no tent
no care what we look like
what we say

Later that night, in my room
looking into the mirror, to tell the truth I was loved
I looked right through into nothing.

Hospice

I wore his hat
as if it was the rumpled coat
of his body, like I could put it on.

The coat of his hair, of his brain, its glitter
he gave it to me, something he'd worn.
He didn't touch his dog, touch was too much,

he didn't let her go.
I felt his hat on my head, like a hand,
though his hat was on the floor, just by my chair.

I went on drinking water
as if there was more water.
I went on living on earth
as if there was still life
on earth

I remembered
like an islander   my island

like a calving iceberg, air

like jazz
rumpled
like its glitter
worn hand
by my chair

*

I thought I'd have to listen, hard,
I didn't even swallow.
But nothing from you stopped.

Isn't there something

Isn't there something in me
like the dogs I've heard at home
who bark all night from hunger? Something
in me like trains leaving,

isn't there something in me
like a gun? I wanted to be
loud squirrels, around the trees' feet,
bees, coming back & back

to the wooden porch,
wanting something—and wooden planks,
wanting something. To go back into
a tree?

I want to go back to you,
who when you were dying said
*There are one or two people you don't want to
let go of.* Here too, where I don't let go of you.

Down on the street

Down on the street
a man's voice, every night at ten—
*God   God   God   I love you   God
Hallelujah   God
Hallelujah   God   God*

Everyone breathing hard to get through,
to get through soon to the air,
a word in everybody's mouth—

You must have trusted some word
that time in that half-underwater cave
when you dove and came up someplace else,
and called to me, *Come on*

Both you & he

Both you & he were there.
I woke up, saw just you,
rumpled cloth hat, eyes closed.
I moved my head, and lost you.

Do I still need to disguise you
in my dream?

Oh north star, disguise what?
My friend,
I can still smell your clothes,
salt, light, the dog, and you.

My words to you

My words to you are the stitches in a scarf
I don't want to finish
maybe it will come to be a blanket
to hold you here

love not gone anywhere

I'm going to sleep

I'm going to sleep now
in case you visit my dream

Full moon   on your left temple
that nickel-size circle of whiter skin
under your straight black hair

I love it specially
as if it is my secret.
From before.

I'd get you a glass of champagne

      if we were still
in that hollow of sand and rock
above the beach. Talking by
listening. It you
were still breathing. *Our purpose
no-purpose.*

We turn in dream

We turn in dream
you to your place
me to mine.

      Across the street from each other
we both turn back.
you wait, short of breath.

I run back across the street,
you wait, your open jacket,
the cars are kind also, & wait.

      God
to be born
into no oxygen
then into breathing.

Are all the things

Are all the things that never happened, OK?
—The wide river at dawn, the hippo's lifted face
—The slow, violet curtains of Antarctic light
(Hide you under the shadow of their wings)

And all the things that came—
the awful, and then love on earth, OK?
my own friend?   where you are?

You're gone

You're gone in the day time
but you're still here at night

I'm going to sleep again
now, just in case

                    not-God, not you quite, either, come
                    —while underground,
your mother bites her wrist-vein
open, to let you drink.

Then

Then no friend, no you
under the subway light   no you

wanting a hand
asking anyone
"Can you help me to speak?"

You Speak

I'm not without you friend
but without stars,
skin & fingers, borders

not separated out. Here
you get past everything
all at once. I remember

everything. That white tree.
And what was never there
to remember, I remember

as if I've come upon
a whole room full of clay books
that I can read with my fingers,

as we once read each other,
younger than water, remember? And
"—if transformation comes?"

I could compare it maybe to a train
in Tolstoy, already having forgiven
everything, forward & backward:

                                              the train is saying
Come on. I'm writing on a tablecloth.
I love you.

408 | Light Me Down: The New & Collected Poems of Jean Valentine

THRESHOLD

Could it be heat?

Could it be heat? Could I be growing out? You my father
in a chair pulled up to the foot of my bed,
rubbing and rubbing my feet, under the blanket.

when I was eleven, when you came back from the war,
Sorry, you said, *I can't speak, it's,*
I'm dead. You rubbed my feet, a hundred years went by.

You sent me away to the library for love.
I found two books: the Window and the Door.
All I did was wait & sleep & write. *Please change. Please open.*

Another hundred years,
The Window opened me.
The Door said, *More.*

The Window:

Did you not suppose I loved you?
I loved you, asleep in the library,
your hair the hue of rain-drenched bark.

But I am little in that world of
home, of bed and chair.
I can't touch there, or see.

I jumped on the subway tracks
when I was seven, they said I fell,
I didn't fall.

They come toward me, a noise starts up
in my ears, an engine of air & kill.

        Can't you understand? I've loved—

—I've loved a woman before this,
in the Philippines, in the war, and then, another,
back here, since.

        There is nothing to open.
Nothing to change.
Now do you understand?

I am a dead tree to the touch.
There is nothing to change.
There is nothing to open.

I love you more, then,
dead tree—you
who open whoever you approach;
you change the comer.

The last time I saw you, it was winter, your hand
held hard to my hand,   you asked
"How long are you here for?"
You bent toward me,

the change in your red lips was death,
cadmium red deep-painted mouth—

When you died, I dreamed
you had fallen asleep on the subway

—Not all that praise laid out on a teak tray
and offered to us to eat,   unhungry.

When I woke up
my clothes were covered with writing,
my hair was sentences, full of twigs,

lines ran between my fingers.
Open, Window, Look, it's
time to fly now.

The owl looked back to me a minute
from the sill: stiff feathers stood
around his eyes: his book.

The Door:

When I first heard you on the phone
your voice had to be that 40s wartime voice
for it to get under my skin like it did,
after seven years asleep.

You're at the beginning of something, you said,
and I'm at the end of something;
but you didn't go away,
twice-born, three times, coming around,
rough cello.

Late days
I want to drive to your grave,
But I don't belong to it.

Shirt in Heaven (2015) | 411

Bellini, Saint Francis

The mountain rocks are blue-green.
The donkey is alone now.
And the crane.
And the rabbit. Next to the book,
the skull. Nothing darkens it.

I know you went blind.
I know you died.
Nothing darkens you, threshold.
Nothing lightens you. You
life unsustainable here   Just about

In the Famine Museum

Don't do that, my mother said,
when I went to put my arm
around her.

So, she said,
you're only here
for a day or two.

We are separate ashes
and bone covered over.
We have a mother, both—our
great-grandmother.
We sit with her
in the Famine Museum
—the begot life—arms
(I don't know how)
around each other's waists.

Great-grandmother, my mother says,
Come for a walk.

Cán the dead walk? she asks.

My mother answers,

—*How not?*

Friend,

you came in a dream yesterday
—The first day we met
you showed me your dark workroom
off the kitchen, your books, your notebooks.

Reading our last, knowing-last letters
—the years of our friendship
reading our poems to each other,
I would start breathing again.

Yesterday, in the afternoon,
more than a year since you died,

some words came into the air.
looked away a second,
and they were gone—
six lines, just passing through.

for Adrienne Rich

Great-grandmother,

be with us
as if in the one same day & night
we all gave birth
in the one same safe-house, warm,
and then we rest together,
sleep, and nurse,
dreamily talk to our babies, warm
in a safe room   all of us
carried in the close black sky.

THEN HAD WE WELL PUT TO,
WITHOUT FORM, WITHOUT TEXT
—Antonin Artaud

Note in winter

Clear window
for now. I,
human animal.
with heat,
& ceiling,
risk.

I gave you
some bad, worn memories.
I know you will not leave,

but risk.

The iron plow
scraping past.
And no snow.

Ten Degrees

From her sidewalk newspaper blanket
she asks for a sandwich.
as if from a mother.

The street has the white
look of winter.
The subways flood.

You have to think with water.

When I woke up, our time

When I woke up, our time was lost. No standing
in physics.   the unconscious.

I washed our friends' old rug
and laid it across the table.

Mandelstam,
the river was shining, silver as a plow.

Your friend, Natasha, the lame girl,
walking ahead, held back her hand
to you on the street:

   —Come on, I've got the rug—

And you said

—Where did I put you
down dear? The world is worse
but I can hear your heart
so steady.   louder.

Someone taken.   Beating a rug.

When I woke up, my friend

When I woke up, my friend
was there with me.
We were on the island
of no going beyond.

Why do they call the dead
the never-returners?

You brought vegetables up from the kitchen,
whistling to let me know
you were approaching the steps.

And even here
two days after you died
we talked on W. 17th Street—

Then everything complicated,
swift & gear.

Self-Portrait, Rembrandt, 1658

I can't look up out of the sadness
only here along with your sadness

In the line of your black hat   the line
around the crown of my head gets stronger
when people come & go between us

From the first time I saw you,
when I was young,
you held me in your own understanding exhaustion.

Song

I was asking pardon, who am I?
Of them who I am: pardon.

Of the slow wearing down
of the window, the sun, I was asking forgiveness,

of the crocodile, that good hider,
of the heron, that good feeder,

& of Christ the pelican.
                    Christ said,

Over a thousand pages of Scripture,
& I was not reading, but dreaming.

It's the same right now, he said.
                         He just stood there.

Shirt in Heaven (2015) | **417**

I, I was not painting, but watching the animals.
I was not copying, but dreaming.

Over one thousand newborns in this clearing. We started
to lick them clean, dreaming, one by one.

Icebergs, Ilulissat

In blue-green air & water God
you have come back for us,
to our fiberglass boat.

You have come back for us, & I'm afraid.
Great sadness at harms.
But nothing now
can be like before.

Even when the icebergs are gone, and the millions of suns
have burnt themselves out of your arms,

your arms of burnt air.

NOTES

NEW POEMS

"To My Teacher" is written for William Alfred.

"Poem with a Line from Ko Un" contains the line "leaving all words behind" from a poem by Ko Un.

"Image:" was retained and contributed by Nancy Mitchell, who received the poem from Jean Valentine.

ORDINARY THINGS

"Autumn Day" "The house in the air. . ."

> Jung's autobiography, *Memories, Dreams, Reflections* (Vintage, recorded and edited by Aniela Jaffé); Chapter X, Visions, These ten pages record Jung's visions during three weeks after his heart attack in 1944. Particularly: "A short distance away I saw in space a tremendous dark block of stone, like a meteorite. It was about the size of my house, or even bigger. It was floating in space, and I myself was floating in space. . .I had the certainty that I was about to enter an illuminated room and would meet there all those people to whom I belong in reality" (pp. 290, 291).

420 | *Light Me Down: The New & Collected Poems of Jean Valentine*

"Revolution": After Pontecorvo's film *Battle of Algiers*.

"Susan's Photograph": "*—even in prison you would have your childhood—*"
Rilke's *Letters to a Young Poet* (W. W. Norton): "And even if you were in some prison the walls of which let none of the sounds of the world come to your senses—would you not then still have your childhood. . . ?" (p. 18).

DOOR IN THE MOUNTAIN

"Annunciation": drawn from Helene Aylon's Breakings.

"Occurrence of White" : the first line echoes Jane Kenyon's poem Things.

Page 308, "My old body":

> My old body
> a drop of dew
> heavy at the leaf tip.
> —Kiba

LITTLE BOAT

"The Eleventh Brother"
  The Wild Swans is by Hans Christian Andersen.
"Remote Objects of Intense Devotion"
  This is a phrase from the Metropolitan Museum's Surrealist Show, describing work by Joseph Cornell.
"The Woman's Poem"
  "Jesus said, Split a piece of wood, and I am there." From The Gospel of Thomas, in The Nag Hammadi Library, James M. Robinson, General Editor, HarperCollins, 1978, 1988.
"The Teacher's Poem"
  Picasso: hearsay.
"Hospital: *At last*"
  This poem is drawn from "Fairies," an essay in *The Wedding Dress*, by Fanny Howe, University of California Press, 2003.

Notes | **421**

"I wanted to be sure to reach you"

This line is from Frank O'Hara's poem "To the Harbormaster"

FROM THE QUESTIONS OF BHANU KAPIL

These questions are from The Vertical Interrogation of Strangers by Bhanu Kapil Rider, Kelsey Street Press, 2002.

"Moose and calf"

"For there within, he showed a place that was inviting fair; and large enough it was to offer refuge for all" is from *Revelation of Love*, by Julian of Norwich, Image Books, 1997.

"To my soul (2)"

The last stanza is drawn from the work of Dorota Mytych.

BREAK THE GLASS

"The branches" is for Jody Gladding.

"Diana": the poem draws on Norman O. Brown's "Metamorphoses II: Actaeon."

"He Disappeared into Complete Silence": Louise Bourgeois, plate 8, 1947.

LUCY:

p.376 - The Holy Bible, King James Version.

p.376 - "my saxifrage that splits the rocks" —see "A Sort of a Song, by William Carlos Williams: "Saxifrage is my flower that splits / the rocks." *The William Carlos Williams Reader*, New Directions, 1966.

p.378 - Nikolay and Ieronim are in Chekhov's story "Easter Eve," in The Bishop and Other Stories, translated by Constance Garnett, The Ecco Press, 1985.

pp.379-380 - Rainer Maria Rilke, Rilke' Book of Hours, translated by Anita Barrows and Joanna Macy, Riverhead Trade, 2005.

p.382 - Martín Ramírez was a Mexican immigrant painter who lived for fifteen years in DeWitt State Hospital in California, until his death in 1963. His work was shown at the American Folk Art Museum in New York City in 2007.

ACKNOWLEDGMENTS

The following sections of this volume were previously published as books:

Dream Barker. Copyright © 1965 by Yale University Press. Reprinted with the permission of Yale University Press.

Pilgrims. Copyright © 1969 by Jean Valentine. First published by Farrar, Straus & Giroux in 1969.

Ordinary Things. Copyright © 1974 by Jean Valentine. First published by Farrar, Straus & Giroux in 1974.

The Messenger. Copyright © 1979 by Jean Valentine. First published by Farrar, Straus & Giroux in 1979.

Home.Deep.Blue. Copyright © 1980 by Jean Valentine. Reprinted with the permission of Alice James Books.

The River at Wolf. Copyright © 1992 by Jean Valentine. Reprinted with permission of Alice James Books.

Growing Darkness, Growing Light. Copyright © 1997 by Jean Valentine. First published by Carnegie Mellon University Press in 1997.

The Cradle of the Real Life. Copyright © 2000 by Jean Valentine. Reprinted with permission of Wesleyan University Press.

Door in the Mountain. Copyright © 2004 by Jean Valentine. Reprinted with permission of Wesleyan University Press.

Little Boat. Copyright © 2007 by Jean Valentine. Reprinted with permission of Wesleyan University Press.

Break the Glass. Copyright © 2010 by Jean Valentine. Reprinted with permission of Copper Canyon Press.

Shirt in Heaven. Copyright © 2015 by Jean Valentine. Reprinted with permission of Copper Canyon Press.

NEW POEMS:

Much gratitude to the individuals who helped collect these poems and to the editors and wonderful people at the following publications for their support of Valentine's final poems, versions of which first appeared as follows:

Field: "Sparrow" and "Trust"

Literary Matters: "The Ring," "Thirst" and "For a friend who died young"

Plume: "In a Diner," "For Tomas Tranströmer & Max Ritvo," "Dear Merton's God," "In Ireland" and "In China"

Still Against the War IX: Poems for Marie Ponsot: "Dear Adrienne"

The Nation: "Yeats' Stance"

The New Yorker: "The Cricket"

The Volta: "A minute of silence for C.D. Wright"

PILGRIMS:

Grateful acknowledgment is made to the following, who first printed some of these poems: Poetry for "The Summer House," "Orpheus and Eurydice," "Separation," "Dearest," "April," "Broken-down Girl," "Archangel," and "Photograph of Delmore Schwartz"; *Yale Review* for "The couples" "By the Boat Pond," and "Thinking About

Cain"; *American Scholar* for "Fireside" (originally "Our Saragasso")' *Commonweal* for "Solomon"; *Radcliffe Quarterly* for "In the Museum"; *The New Yorker* for "The Torn-down Building"; *Colloquy* for "Moon Man" and "Visiting Day at School" (read as the Phi Beta Kappa poem at Swarthmore College in June, 1968); and to Random House, publisher of Olga Carlisle's *Poets on Street Corners*, in whose pages the Ahkmadulina adaptation, "Goodbye," originally appeared.

THE MESSENGER:

Some of the poems in this collection first appeared—at times in different versions—in *The American Poetry Review; Blacksmith Anthology*, edited by Gail Mazur; *Field; Green House; Harvard Magazine; Ironwood; The Nation; The New Yorker* ("Beka, 14"; "The Messenger"); *Pequod; Pocket Pal; Transatlantic Review; Vanderbilt Review*.

Seven of the poems in the first part were printed as a chapbook, Turn, edited by Bruce Weigl, designed by Jean Kondo Weigl, Pocket Pal Press, Oberlin, Ohio, 1977.

I want to thank the John Simon Guggenheim Memorial Foundation for the grant which gave me the freedom to finish this book. And—again—my thanks to Yaddo, and to The MacDowell Colony, for their space and quiet.

The poem by Huub Oosterhuis was translated with Judith Herzberg.

The poem by Osip Mandelstam was translated with Anne Frydman.

HOME.DEEP.BLUE:

Some of the new poems in this collection first appeared in *The American Poetry Review; Antaeus; The Barat Review; Boulevard; Field; Ironwood; The New Yorker* ("Visit"; "The Counselor Retires and Then He Dies"; "Everything Starts with a Leter", "The King"); *The Paris Review; Poetry Miscellany*.

To them, once again to the MacDowell Colony, and to Peter Schumann and the Bread and Puppet Theater for the Masonite-cut on the cover of this book, my heartfelt thanks.

THE RIVER AT WOLF:

Some of these poems were originally published in the following magazines:

The American Poetry Review: "The Year of the Snake," "The One You Wanted to Be Is

426 | *Light Me Down: The New & Collected Poems of Jean Valentine*

the One You Are," "Ironwood," "Bud," "To a Young Poet," "Foraging," "Alfred and the Abortion," "Redemption," "Seeing You," "The Free Abandonment Blues," "The First Station," "The Night Lake," "In Fear," "The Under Voice," "Come Ahkmatova," "Wish-Mother," "American River Sky Alcohol Father" and "Second Mother"

The American Voice: "X" and "Still Life, for Matisse"

Boulevard: "Spring and Its Flowers"

The Brooklyn Review: "Flower"

Field: "Still Life: in the Epidemic," "Ikon," "The Ring," "James Wright: in Memory," "At My Mother's Grave," "The First Angel" and "Yield Everything, Force Nothing"

Folio: "At Cullens' Island"

Hayden's Ferry Review: "Butane," "At the Door" and "My Mother's Body, My Professor, My Bower"

The New Yorker: "The Summer Was Not Long Enough," "The Badlands Said," "The River at Wolf," "Barrie's Dream, the Wild Geese," "The Wisdom Gravy" and "The Sea of Serenity"

Ploughshares: "Fox Glacier" and "By the Tekapo River, 100 Degrees"

The Plum Review: "Lindis Pass, Borage" and "The Morning of My Mother's Death"

Princetown Arts: "The Missouri Speaks," "Everyone Was Drunk" and "This Egg"

The Southern California Anthology: "After Consciousness of This Big Form" and "The Night of My Mother's Death"

To them, and to the MacDowell Colony and the UCross Foundation, my deepest thanks.

THE CRADLE OF THE REAL LIFE:

Grateful acknowledgment is made to the following periodicals in which these poems first appeared: *American Poetry Review, Boston Book Review, Controlled Burn, Field, Global City Review, Hayden's Ferry Review, Kenyon Review, Massachusetts Review, Painted Leaf Press, Provincetown Arts, Ruah, Salamander, Southern Review,* and *Third Bed.* To the editors, and to the MacDowell Colony, Yaddo, and Dorland Mountain, my deep thanks.

DOOR IN THE MOUNTAIN:

Grateful acknowledgment is made to the following periodicals in which the poems in *Door in the Mountain* first appeared: *American Poetry Review, Arts & Letters, Barrow Street, Boston Book Review, <canwehaveourballback.com>, Hayden's Ferry, Heliotrope,*

Acknowledgments | **427**

Kestrel, Luna, Massachusetts Review, The New Yorker ("Sheep," "My old body," "One Foot in the Dark"); *Ohio Review, Persephone, Poetry Ireland, Two Rivers, U.S. I Worksheets, van Goh's Ear, Virginia Quarterly Review, and Washington Square Review.*

Also to the following anthologies: *Best American Poems 2002, Blood and Tears: Poems for Matthew Shepard, The Book of Irish American Poetry, Hammer and Blaze,* and *Poetry After 9/11.*

To the editors, and to Dorland Mountain, The MacDowell Colony, and Yaddo, my deep thanks.

LITTLE BOAT:

Grateful acknowledgment is made to the following periodicals in which poems in Little Boat first appeared: *American Poetry Review, Apocryphaltext, Black Clock, Columbia Journal, Columbia Poetry Review, Court Green, crazyhorse, Field, Five AM, Hotel Amerika, Hunger Mountain, Kestrel, Lumina, Lyric, The New Yorker* ("To My Soul"), *Octopus, Pleiades, Pool,* and *Salamander.* "The Artist in Prison" was made into a broadside for Kent State University by Eric May. "How will you/ have you prepare(d) for your death?" was made into a broadside for Columbia College Chicago by April Sheridan. The sequence "Strange Lights" was made into a chapbook for The Center for Book Arts (2005) by Roni Gross, with drawings by Peter Schell.

To the editors, and to the Blue Mountain Center, the MacDowell Colony, and the Virginia Center for the Creative Arts, my deep thanks. And I want to thank, for their loving kindness to me and to this book, Kaveh Bassiri, Myra Goldberg, Kate and Max Greenstreet, Joan Larkin, Anne Marie Macari, and Stephanie Smith.

BREAK THE GLASS:

Alaska Quarterly Review, The American Poetry Review, Blackbird, Chicago Review, The Cortland Review, Field, Great River Review, The Laurel Review, The Massachusetts Review, Narrative, The Nation, The New Yorker, PMS, Poetry International, upstreet.

"Lucy" was published in Sarabande Books' Quarternote Chapbook Series in 2009.

Heartfelt gratitude to Kaveh Bassiri, Sarah Heller, Joan Larkin, Jan Heller Levi, Jack Lynch, Anne Marie Macari, and Stephanie Smith; to and to everyone at the MacDowell Colony, Ucross, and at Sarabande Books and Copper Canyon Press.

428 | *Light Me Down: The New & Collected Poems of Jean Valentine*

SHIRT IN HEAVEN:

The American Poetry Review, The Boston Review, Faultline, Field, Fifth Wednesday, Gwarlingo, Ibbetson Street Magazine, la petite zine, Little Star, Martha's Vineyard Arts and Ideas, Plume, St. Petersburg Review, Spacecraft, Spoon River Poetry Review
Deep thanks to Janet Kaplan of Red Glass Books for printing "The Ship" and to Brian Teare for printing "Friend" in Albion Books.
The poem "God of Rooms" was published in *Homage to Paul Celan*, edited by Ilya Kaminsky & G.C. Waldrep.
Deep thanks to Peter Shumann & the Bread & Puppet Theater for Shirt in Heaven, the masonite-cut on the cover, and also for the book's title.
With heartfelt gratitude to everyone at the Lannan Foundation, the MacDowell Colony, VCCA, Vermont Studio Center, to Jaime Shearn Coan, and to the horses.

INDEX OF TITLES

A

A Bit of Rice, 236
A Bone Standing Up, 287
About Love, 173
Abortion Child, 276
A Bride's Hours, 43
A Child's Death, 107
A Child's Drawing, 1941, 387
"Actuarial File", 154
Adam and Eve: Poem on
    Folded Paper, 63
Advent Calendar, 314
Afterbirth, 45
After Consciousness of
    This Big Form, 199
After Elegies, 101
After Elegies (2), 104
After Elegies (3), 134
After Fernando Traverso, 28
Alcohol, 234
A leaf, a shadow-hand, 396
Alfred and the Abortion, 189
All around the outside, 333
Alone, Alive, 213
American River Sky Alcohol
    Father, 205
A minute of silence for C.D. Wright, 26
Anesthesia, 104
Annunciation, 283
Annunciation Poem, 335

April, 83
Archangel, 87
Are all the things, 406
Asleep over Lines from
    Willa Cather, 38
"As with rosy steps the morn", 354
At Cullens' Island, 204
At My Mother's Grave, 209
At the Conference on Women in the
    Academy, 268
At the Door, 212
'Autumn Day', 101
Avalon, 313
Awake, This Summer, 165
Away from you, 265
A weed green, 310

B

Bardo, 394
Barrie's Dream, the Wild Geese, 197
Bees, 223
Beka, 14, 125
Bellini, Saint Francis, 411
Bin Dream #2, Interview with
    Stravinsky, 85
Bin Dream, West College East, D-II, 85
Birthday Letter from South
    Carolina, 167
Black for the People, 230
Black Wolf, 252

Both you & he, 403
Broken-down Girl, 84
Bud, 187
Bury your money, 399
Butane, 209
But your touch, 325
By the Boat Pond, 74
By the Tekapo River, 100 Degrees, 199

C

Cambridge, April 27, 1957, 47
Cambridge by Night, 39
Canoe, 356
Child, 266
Coltrane, Syeeda's Song Flute, 90
Come Ahkmatova, 203
Could it be heat?, 408
Cousin, 289
Couvre-Feu: after Paul Eluard, 118
Coyote, 359

D

Day & Night, 333
Dear Adrienne, 8
Dearest, 82
Dear Family, 355
Dear Merton's God, 20
Death Asphodel, 210
Death House, 86
Death Poem, 336
December 21st, 143
Desert Prison, 370
Diana, 373
Documentary: AIDS Support
    Group, 235

Do flies remember us, 297
Dog Skin Coat, 232
Don't silence yourself, No te calles, 367
Door, 328
Door in the Mountain, 307
Down on the street, 403
Do you remember?, 314
Dream Barker, 67
Dufy Postcard, 125
Déjà-vu, 37

E

Earth and the Librarian, 361
Eighteen, 285
Elegy for Jane Kenyon, 233
Elegy for Jane Kenyon (2), 251
Eleventh Brother, 291
Embryo, 266
Eurydice who guides, 367
Even all night long, 253
Everyone Was Drunk, 200
Everything Starts with a Letter, 172
Eye of water, 347

F

Father Lynch Returns from
    the Dead, 238
Fears: Night Cabin, 310
February, 2017, 16
February 9th, 150
Fellini in Purgatory, 233
Fidelities, 119
Fireside, 71
First Love, 33
Fistula, 242

Index of Titles | **433**

Flower, 214

For a friend who died young, 23

Foraging, 188

For a Woman Dead at Thirty, 33

For a Women Dead at Thirty (2), 260

Forces, 103

Forces (2): Song, 122

Forest, Stars, 388

For her, 323

For love, 392

For Monty, 25

For Teed, 50

For Tomas Tranströmer &
      Max Ritvo, 15

Fox Glacier, 198

Friend, 222

Friend, 412

G

Ghost Elephants, 357

Go Clear, 293

God of rooms, 389

Goodbye, 79

Gray, 329

Great-grandmother, 413

Green for the Land, 229

Guardian Angel in New York, 215

H

Half an Hour, 87

Happiness, 264

Happiness (2): The I Ching, 264

Happiness (3), 298

Hawkins Stable, 360

He Disappeared into

Complete Silence, 374

He leaves them:, 265

He says to Me, In Ireland, 269

Her car, 262

Her dream: the child, 77

Here, 29

Here Now, 128

Her last year, 389

He said, 102

High School Boyfriend, 175

His hand takes, 398

His White Jade Eggs, 342

Hold the finch, 390

Home, 231

Home, 277

Homesick, 222

Hospice, 401

Hospital: At last, 337

Hospital: far from home, 337

Hospital: It was euphoria, 339

Hospital: Scraps, 339

Hospital: strange lights, 338

How have I hurt you?, 296

How will you/have you prepare(d) for
      your death?, 346

Huub Oosterhuis: Orpheus, 139

I

I am fain a page in the court
      of space, 375

I came to you, 288

I cannot write about it., 400

Icebergs, Ilulissat, 417

I could never let go, 299

I dropped a plate, 369

If a Person Visits Someone in a Dream,

in Some Cultures the Dream
Thanks Them, 360
I have lived in your face, 311
I heard my left hand, 294
Ikon, 185
Image:, 5
In a Diner, 14
In China, 22
In Fear (1), 201
In Fear (2), 201
In Ireland, 21
Inkwell daybreak, 308
In Memory, 324
In our child house, 283
In prison, 357
Inside, 316
In the Burning Air, 318
In the evening, 294
In the Famine Museum, 411
In the Museum, 73
In the Public Library, 267
In This Egg, 201
In your eyes, 302
Ironwood, 187
Isn't there something, 402
I thought It's time, 372
I wanted to be sure to reach you, 340
I was lying there, 342
I was working, 354
I would be, 313
I'd get you a glass of champagne, 405
I'm going to sleep, 404

J

James Wright: in Memory, 203
Juliana, 169

K

Kin, 103

L

Labrador, 256
La Chalupa, the Boat, 323
Leaving, 258
Letter, 299
Letter from a Country Room, 106
Letter from a Stranger, 154
Light Me Down, 1
Lindis Pass, Borage, 198
Lines from a Story, 156
Lines in Dejection, 36
Listening, 245
Little house, 218
Little Map, 262
Little Song in Indian Summer, 174
Living Together, 127
Long Irish Summer Day, 231
Lord of the world!, 327
"Love and Work": Freud Dying, 153
Luna Moth, 287

M

Mandelstam, 166
March 21st, 157
Mare and Newborn Foal, 254
Margaret, d. 1985, 267
Maria Gravida, 346
Mastectomy, 227
Mattress on the floor:, 327
Miles from Home, 34
Monarch butterfly, 307

Index of Titles | **435**

Moon Man, 93
Moose and calf, 347
Mother, 285
Mother and Child, Body
    and Soul   , 239
Mother Bones, 253
My Grandmother's Watch, 51
My Mother's Body, My Professor,
    My Bower, 208
My old body, 308
My words to you, 404

N

New Life, 223
New York, April 27, 1962, 48
Night, 95
Night Lake, 194
Night Porch, 224
Nine, 283
Noon in the Line Outside, 315
Note in winter, 413
November, 256

O

Occurrence of White, 296
October morning, 294
October Premonition, 255
Old love, I want to phone you, 373
On a Passenger Ferry, 358
Once, 290
Once in the nights, 291
Once I was girls and boys, 330
One Foot in the Dark, 310
On the bus, 365
On the CD, in the rainstorm, 372

Open, 395
Open Heart, 243
Orpheus and Eurydice, 77
Osip Mandelstam: 394, 141
Out in a sailboat, 287
Outside the Frame, 122

P

Peace to bad waters, 393
Photograph of Delmore Schwartz, 91
Photographs at her Wake, 326
Pilgrims, 96
Pneumonia, January, 7
Poem with a Line from Ko Un, 19
Poem with endwords by Reginald
    Shepherd, 399
Poem with Words by
    Thornton Dial, 235
Poet, 363
Poetry, 272
Prayer in Fever, 131
Primitive Painting: Liberation Day, 164

R

Radio: Poetry Reading, NPR, 259
Rain, 221
Reading the Mandelstams, 269
Red cloth, 366
Redemption, 190
Red for Blood, 228
"Regard all dharmas as dreams", 24
"Remote Objects of Intense
    Devotion", 331
Revolution, 108
River Jordan, 224

Riverside, 49
Rodney Dying, 237
Rodney Dying (2), 237
Rodney Dying (3), 256
Rodney Dying (4), 306
Running for a train, 258

S

Sanctuary, 144
Sarah's Christening Day, 46
Sasha and the Poet, 43
Second Mother, 207
Secret Room, Danger House, 228
Seeing L'Atalante, 110
Seeing You, 191
Self-Portrait, Rembrandt, 1658, 416
Separation, 79
September 1963, 49
Sex, 63
Sheep, 305
"She Sang", 286
She will be, 400
Shirt in Heaven, 392
Sick, Away from Home, 221
Silences: A Dream of Governments, 133
Single Mother, 1966, 276
Skate, 214
Sleep Drops Its Nets, 37
Snow Family, 226
Snow Landscape, in a Glass Globe, 171
Solomon, 72
So many secrets, 290
Song, 416
Soul, 240
Soul (2), 240
Soul (3), 242

so wild, 311
Space, 105
Sparrow, 12
Spring and Its Flowers, 181
Still Life, for Matisse, 183
Still Life: in the Epidemic, 183
Sunset at Wellfleet, 38
Susan's Photograph, 121

T

Tell Me, What Is the Soul, 227
Ten Degrees, 414
That I had treated you badly, 332
The 40's, 18
The Afterlife Poem, 336
The Artist in Prison, 324
The Baby Rabbits in the Garden, 238
The Badlands Said, 195
The Basket House, 300
The Beast with Two Backs, 52
The Blind Stirring of Love, 261
The Blue Dory, the Soul, 304
The branches, 366
The Burden of Memory, 148
The Child and the Terrorist,
    The Terrorist and the Child, 94
The Child Jung, 90
The Church, 273
The Coin, 293
The Counselor Retires, and Then
    He Dies, 168
The Couples, 71
The Cricket, 11
The Door:, 410
The door is fallen down, 328
The Drinker, 262

Index of Titles | **437**

The Drinker (2), 263

The Drinker's Wife Writes Back, 167

The Eleventh Brother (2), 330

The father was a carrier, 329

The Field, 126

The First Angel, 211

The First Station, 193

The first thing, 332

The Forgiveness Dream: Man from the
Warsaw Ghetto, 129

The Free Abandonment Blues, 192

The girl, 284

The grain of the wood, 312

The Growing Christ of
Tzintzuntzan, 305

The Harrowing, 343

The Hawthorn Robin Mends
with Thorns, 287

The helicopter, 397

The House and the World, 301

The Japanese garden, 356

The just-born rabbits, 364

The King, 174

The Knife, 109

The Leopard, 352

The little, faintly blue clay eggs, 298

The Little Flower, 54

The Locked Ward: O.T., 275

The Longing, 17

The Look, 340

The Messenger, 135

The Missouri Speaks, 195

The Morning of My Mother's
Death, 206

The Mother Dreams, 241

Then, 406

Then Abraham, 358

The Needle North, 317

The Night of My Mother's Death, 206

The Night of Wally's Service,
Wally Said, 236

The Night Sea, 309

The older man among us, 374

The One You Wanted to Be Is the One
You Are, 186

The Orphanage Landing, 268

The Passing, 317

The path between, 308

The Pen, 251

The Poet, 326

The Poet's Poem, 335

The Power Table, 216

The Prison, 27

The push or fly, 312

The Rally, 304

there's nothing when, 393

The Ring, 2

The Ring, 197

The River at Wolf, 196

The Rose, 348

The Sea of Serenity, 208

The Second Dream, 43

[The ship] is slowly giving up
her sentient life,
I cannot write about it., 400

The Shirt, 309

The Summer House, 75

The Summer Was Not Long
Enough, 182

The Teacher, 10

The Teacher's Poem, 336

The Torn-down Building, 92

The Tower Roof, 260

The Tractors, 223

The treeless hill, 364
The Under Voice, 202
The valley, 365
The Very Bad Horse, 289
The Welsh poet, 259
The whitewashed walls, 352
The Window:, 408
The Windows, 292
The Wisdom Gravy, 205
The Woman's Poem, 334
The Women's Prison, 267
The World inside This One, 362
The Year of the Snake, 185
They lead me, 253
The Young Mother, 371
Thinking about Cain, 82
Thirst, 4
This Hate, 115
This Minute, 116
This Side, 341
Three Voices One Night in the
    Community Kitchen, 108
Time is matter here, 361
Tired of London, 46
To a Friend, 40
To a Young Poet, 188
To Ireland, 276
To My Soul, 65
To my soul (2), 348
To My Teacher, 3
Tonight I Can Write . . ., 175
To Plath, to Sexton, 215
To Raphael, angel of
    happy meeting, 163
To Salter's Point, 35
To the Bardo, 306
To the Black Madonna of Chartres, 226

To the Memory of David Kalstone, 211
Touch with your finger, 315
Traveler, 359
Trim my hoofs, 302
Trust, 13
Trust me, 6
Trust Me, 176
Truth, 255
Turn, 130
Turn (2): After Years, 147
Twenty Days' Journey, 111
Two Poems for Matthew Shepard, 303
(Two were seen leaving.), 363

U

Under the gold, 291

V

Visit, 170
Visiting Day at School, 89

W

W. 13th Street, 395
Waiting, 41
We cut the new day, 295
We didn't know each other, 315
We Go Through Our Mother's
    Things, 210
We turn in dream, 405
What are the consequences
    of silence?, 345
What do you remember about
    the earth?, 345
What God Said, 270

Index of Titles | **439**

What Happened, 145
What is the shape of your body?, 344
When I lost my courage, 398
When I woke up, my friend, 415
When I woke up, our time, 414
When she told me, 341
Where did you come from/how did
    you arrive?, 344
Where Do You Look for Me?, 235
Who watches, 360
Willi, Home, 163
Wish-Mother, 204
Woman, Leaving, 302
Woods, 76
Working, 132
World-light, 225

X

X, 181

Y

Yeats' Stance, 9
Yellow for Gold, 229
Yield Everything, Force Nothing, 212
You Are Not One in a Sequence, 234
You ask,, 317
You drew my head, 297
Your mouth "appeared to me", 254
Your number is lifting off my hand, 316
You rope that pulls them where they
    do not go, 396
You Speak, 407
You're gone, 406

Numbered Titles

3 A.M. in New York, 105
1943: The Vision, 388
1945, 257
1945, 291

INDEX OF FIRST LINES

A

A bit of rice in a string bag:, 236
A bone standing up, 287
After she died, 270
A goldfinch in the rain, 312
A guy smoking, in his chair, 331
A homeless woman with harsh
    white hair, 203
a labyrinth, 348
A leaf, a shadow-hand, 396
Alfred, what did they do with your
    arm bones?, 189
All around the outside of the room
    I was given, 333
All night long I listened to the coal
    train, 345
All the years waiting, the whole,
    barren, young, 63
All this anger, 301
All this from the world, 19
Almost two years now I've been
    sleeping, 101
(Alone), 264
Alone, alive, 213
A lorry scatters, 231
A MAN:, 108
A man whose arms and shoulders, 223
A man with an infant in his lap, 242
A matchbox painted and figured, 359
And finally I'll say goodbye., 79
And inside them   deep space, 363
An imaginary mother, 334

April 6th: the country thaws
    and drips, 50
A quilt of mothers and children:, 345
Are all the things that never
    happened, OK?, 406
A sculpture in a bare white gallery:, 126
Ask, and let your words diminish
    your asking, 41
A spit of sky, awash with Venetian
    gold, 38
At a memorial service, 234
A thumbnail-sized globe of blood:, 206
A thumb's length landscape: Snow, on
    a hill, 171
At the back of the church, 267
At the library, 361
Avalon, 313
Away, I dream, 25
Away from you, 265
A weed   green, 310
A woman's face at the window, 103
A woman ladder leans, 387
A woman sits at her workable,
    reading stories, 110
A woman was picking up
    the plastic, 306
A year in the Pacific, 257
A young king, 91

B

B. is dragging his mother's bones, 253
B. walks around with a fire-box inside

his chest., 223

Back home, after a month away, 224

Because why—I was dis-, 229

Begging my mother to speak
to him, 229

Being told, 209

be with us, 413

Black hair, 207

Both you & he were there., 403

Breath entering, leaving the leaf, 231

Brown museum hair, brushed the way
they brush it there, 380

—But to go away!, 340

But what about the blue dory—
the soul, 303

But your touch was everywhere,
Lord, 325

By the Granary River, 276

By the St. Vrain River, 201

C

Child, 239

Christmas night, my father said,
"Jean, 187

Clear window, 413

Come in, 305

Come upon a snapshot, 392

Coming east we left the animals, 196

Could it be heat? Could I be growing
out? You my father, 408

Could we have coffee? —No,
my truth, 371

Crossing a fenced-off railroad
track, 256

D

Dancing in a room full of muzak
and smoke, 237

Dawn, streaks of rose-brown,
dry—, 127

Day & night, 333

Day by day you are being drawn, 235

Dearest, what were you doing there
tonight?, 338

Dearest darling woodenhead, 76

Dear life, 16

Dear Reginald, 368

The treeless hill that gave holes, 364

Did you not suppose I loved you?, 408

Do flies remember us, 297

Don't do that, my mother said, 411

Door, 328

Do well in the world., 225

Down on the street, 403

Down the aisles of this dark town, 39

Do you remember, last time we s
aw each other, how the first
thing, 148

Do you remember? my mouth black
and blue, 314

driftwood   seaweed, 393

Drink   cut my wrists, 274

E

Eimear was dead:, 204

Eurydice who guides   Orpheus
who guides, 367

Even all night long while, 353

Everyone, 354

Everyone is wearing work clothes, old

Index of First Lines | **443**

clothes, boots; and old uni-, 164
Everything starts with a letter, 172
Excursion: a night, two days, 52

F

Fat slippery angels, 211
First thriving, then failing
    to thrive:, 296
For her, 323
Friend I need your hand every
    morning, 222
Friend or no friend, 226
From her sidewalk newspaper
    blanket, 414
From this night on God let me eat, 95
From Tipperary.   In swaddling
    clothes., 344
From your eyes I thought, 133
Funeral dream, 292

G

Getting each other's jokes, 168
Go clear   he said, 293
God of rooms, of this room made of
    taken-away, 389
Goosedown on the warm curve of a
    pail., 205
"Gossip is travel, 85
Gray, 329
Green bookbag full of poems, 285
Grown, and miles from home, why do
    I shy, 34

H

He could watch his soul, a line
    drawing, almost a cartoon,
    rise up, 153
He leaves them:, 265
He looked about six or seven, only
    much too thin., 129
He must have been one or two,
    I was five, 194
Her car had hit another car., 362
Here, 234
Here in Framingham, black,
    unlikely, 35
Here in the close, most clear sun, 134
Here is a man., 108
Here's the letter I wrote, 211
He says to me, In Ireland, 269
He took some words from the bowl, 367
He was shoveling sand, 233
His hand takes after me with
    a knife., 398
Hold the finch who flew into the
    window, 390
horse running sideways, 396
How deep we met in the sea,
    my love, 33
How have I hurt you?, 296
How will I think of you, 143
Hunger of the tongue, 326
Hurt, hurtful, snake-charmed, 87

I

I'm standing there, 363
I am, 174
I am the razor that has been put

away, also, 121
I am the skull, 195
I am twenty, 323
I cannot give you much or ask
    you much., 40
I came to you, 288
I can't look up out of the sadness, 416
I don't know what happened, some
    very low time for my friend;, 145
"I dreamed about Elizabeth Bishop, 197
I dreamed I finally got through to C on
    the phone, 306
I dreamed two nights ago, 7
I dropped a plate and broke it, 369
— I feel like I've buried somebody
    inside of me, 210
If every present is possible, 370
if we were still, 405
I had a boat, 317
I had to ask you questions: if I didn't,
    well, 185
I have been standing at the edge, 105
I have lived in your face., 311
I have nay ben nn, 347
I have pulled the elements in
    no order, 375
I heard my left hand love for my
    right hand, 294
I heard your voice on the radio, 259
I lay down under language, 395
I left my clothes, 277
—I left the blue dory, 304
I loiter in the eye of the Slough, 45
I looked, 15
Imagine her quick, 84
I miss another body in this life.
    But miss, 373

In blue-green air & water God, 417
I needed a friend but, 338
Inkwell   daybreak, 308
In memory, 260
In my first hour, the thirst
    was for air, 4
In my sleep:, 109
In our child house, 283
In prison, 351
In the burning air, 318
In the doorway, 263
In the elephant field, 357
In the evening, 294
In the library, 10
In the Public Library, 267
In the strange house, 135
In the tiny window for
    December 21st, 314
In this little borrowed, 11
In your eyes, 302
in your white dress, 285
I remember the dark spaces, 107
I rub my hands my cheeks, 261
I saw a table on the sidewalk, 395
I saw it when I was nine, 388
I saw it—there's, 399
I saw my soul become flesh   breaking
    open, 283
I saw streaming up out of the sidewalk
    the homeless women and, 202
I see you a minute, a year ago, at the
    door, 165
I sit across from him—, 14
Isn't there something in me, 402
Is the train I'm on, moving?   or
    is it, 342
It's a piece of brown wrapping

Index of First Lines | **445**

paper, 379
It's dark in here, 87
I thank God, I have never taken to
    drinking, as many I know
    have, I, 54
I thought:, 276
I thought   it's only a thin
    threshold, 111
I thought It's time to go into the forest
    with a bowl., 372
I thought my wearing out my shoes
    on poems, 335
It is enough, now, anywhere, 122
It is like a fitting room only, 115
I try to hold you face in my mind's
    million eyes, 43
It stared and stared, 77
It was euphoria, 339
It was the same kind of night, the light,
    the coughing, 86
It was years before you could
    climb, 360
I vacuumed your bedroom, 256
I was asking pardon, who am I?, 416
I was born under the mudbank, 191
I was lying there, half-alive, 342
I was over at your place, 324
I was working on cleaning
    up a house, 354
I wear this ring, 2
I will trade, 324
I wore his hat, 401
I would be thick soft fleece, 313
I—as daughter—am black:, 240
I'm going to sleep now, 404
I'm not without you friend, 407
I'm with D. and a young woman, 241

I've never felt, 204

J

Jane is big, 251
January. At the window, 147
Jesus said, 336
Jesus said, 336
Jesus said, Fix anything—, 336
Jonathan, 195

K

Keeping to my room, 105

L

Last night, just before sleep, this: a
    bright, 163
Leonardo's man in the circle, but a
    woman, 222
Light, 183
Light, 183
Light me down to the long meadow, 1
Like a leopard on a shield, the
    space leopard, 352
Listen to the crescent, 358
Little house, 318
Looking back at me, 203
Lord of the world!   Soft, 327
Lucy, whose skeleton is approximately
    3.2 million years, 375
Luna moth, 387
Lying in a bunk on a train, 240
Lynda, the third, last time
    we talked, 232

M

M. comes and hits me, 201
Martín Ramírez, 382
Mary, 198
Milk called out of the breast, 371
Monarch butterfly, 307
Moose and calf eat the shoots of the
    willow trees, 347
"Most people will reflect back
    to you, 236
Mother   your quiet face, 156
—my silky bed for you, 335
My first own half-grown tenderness, 3
My first own home, 289
My head, 221
my husband, 299
My mother as a child, 201
My mother's house, 166
My old body:, 308
my protectors blue, 327
My sister comes around the corner
    of the house, 228
My whole life I was swimming
    listening, 245
My words to you are the stitches
    in a scarf, 404

N

Nan, the poet in Rome, New York,
    yesterday, 190
Never ran this hard through
    the valley, 307
NI UNO, NI OTRO, 28
No, my father here, as You said, 37
No money, 276

No music, 260
No one ever talked like that before,
    like your, 33
No time alone   sun   rain, 337
November, 256
November 17th, 187
November 1862. Dear Family, 355
Now, there: there's the money., 399
Now, with March forcing our brittle
    spines like first childbirth, 49
Now a year after your death, fish-
    mother, skate, 214
No   when you went to her, 173
Now I don't have to leave this place not
    for anybody, 192
Now I lay me desolate to sleep, 38
Now the stars didn't show:, 388

O

October morning—, 294
October premonition, 255
Off without you, 106
OK my child, 79
O mud mother lick me before I die, 224
Once in the nights, 291
Once I was girls and boys — now, 330
Once there was a woodcutter, 290
one arm still a swan's wing, 291
One night they all, 71
On the CD, in the rainstorm, 372
Orange peels, burned letters, the car
    lights shining on the grass, 155
Orpheus like a farmer, 139
Our great-aunt Frances's look, trust, 13
Our Lord, today is Sarah's
    christening day., 46

Our lives went differently, 169
—Our mother laid us there, 238
Out in a sailboat with the warden, 287
Out the window, 18

P

Pain took me, but, 340
People forget, 310
Poster paints, big brushes, 275

Q

quiet.   ready, 346

R

R, is sitting in a draft, 237
Red cloth, 366
Remember how we spread our hair
    on the sea, 37
Remember our happiness?, 264
Remember we sat by your window
    and smoked, 8
Rest your mouth., 389
Right after her birth they
    crowded in, 104
Running for a train, 258

S

Sam and I chose a workshop called, 199
Sasha: I dreamed you and he, 43
Save the goat of humanity!, 286
Scattered milkweed, valentine, 65
Scraps of hard feelings, 339
Seeing my daughter in the circle

of lamplight, 212
—Secret Room, Danger House:, 228
Shackleton, diary, 400
Sharing bread, 255
She saying, You don't have to do
    anything, 186
She took his hand, 75
She will be, 400
Sleep drops its nets for monsters old
    as the Flood; 37
Slowly, slowly our exploding time, 92
Snakes of water and light in the
    window, 221
Snake   tick, 310
Snow falling the sixth night, 269
Snow family: big snow father, 226
So many secrets, 290
Sometimes, 29
South Dakota, August 1989. The
    buffaloes' deep red-brown, 200
So what use was poetry, 215
so wild, 311
spills the half-gallon of milk on
    the floor., 284
Squat, slant-eyed, speaking in phrase-
    book phrases, the messenger, 125
Standing there they began to grow
    skins, 96
Stanley, my ex, the painter, 182
Staunch meadows for the children, 344
Steamer trunks, 362
Still, gold, open-handed, 72
Still mermaid, 266
Suffocated in the country, 252
Suppose we are standing together
    a minute, 83
Swim in you, sleep, 185

Swimming down to us, 93

T

Talking with Mary about 1972:, 287
"Thank you for the food," we said, 273
That I had treated you badly, 332
The basket house:, 300
The blood rushing under her, 242
The boatpond, broken off, looks back
    at the sky., 181
The branches looked first like
    tepees, 366
The car you were driving, 330
The consolation of another solitude,
    miles away, years away; in, 150
The dark black line, 258
The deck is big, and crowded. In one
    corner, 358
The doctors tell me, "Swim., 104
The door is fallen down, 328
The erotic brown fedora on
    the desk:, 289
The father was a carrier, 329
The first life's blood. Now day, 82
The first silver work of kindness, 193
The first thing this guy takes, 332
The fox went under the garden, 71
the ghost-bus travels along
    beside us, 365
The globe's on fire in his hands, 94
The grain of the wood, 312
The grave window-eyes across the
    street, 341
The gray slate roof for hair, 27
The helicopter, 397
The hornet holds on to the

curtain, winter, 299
The hospital shuts down to its half-
    night., 131
The house in the air is rising, not, 101
The huge aluminum airship, 209
The Japanese garden, 356
The just-born rabbits in
    the garden, 364
The lion retreats from the cage
    we can see, 243
The little, faintly blue clay eggs, 298
The longing for touch, 309
The longing is gone to know you,
    God, 17
The man I am with is black, 230
The moment you turned to me on
    W. 4th St., 298
The mountain rocks are
    blue-green., 411
Then, *Tell me your fantasies*,
    you said., 181
Then an old man came down out of
    the thicket, 358
The newspapers blowing over
    the street, 74
The night of my mother's death:, 206
Then no friend, no you, 406
Then the gold mother began her
    touching me, 346
The older man among us looked right
    through me. Lost., 374
The path between the two twelve-foot
    hedges, 308
The pear tree buds shine like salt;, 163
The postcard taped on your white
    kitchen wall has roses, in
    a white, 125

Index of First Lines | 449

The pretty woman with a prisoner number, CDCP *****, written in, 315
The prophets shade their eyes, 26
The push or fly of the snow, 312
The rally is about a young black man, 304
There is a prison room, 227
there's nothing when you're young and clare, 393
There's one day a year, 238
The ring was, 197
The rooks rise off the field in a black W, 233
The sandy road, the bright green two-inch lizard, 251
The Sea of Serenity:, 208
The shimmer, 317
The shirt was going to be red:, 309
The sky is the same changing, 128
The tab on the tea bag said, 373
The tall, good, raw-boned, wrong, 89
The Tourist: Blue plough bones, 198
The tractors at night, 223
The valley, 365
The videotape runs, 116
The Welsh poet, 259
The white pine, 262
The whitewashed walls, the chair, 352
The wild ladders of longing, 374
The winter trees offer no shade no shelter., 391
The women in the prison, 267
The worn hands, 343
They lead me to a, 253
The young scholar, her weeping finger, 268

There is a stone, 73
They think because I am dead now, 235
They used to make a new breast for you, 227
this day broke, 82
This is the new apartment   new, 130
This January night at ten below I wish you, 188
This man, blind and honored, 103
"This stone is, 90
This warm house, masculine; our old, 170
Time is matter here, 361
To Marilyn, to Peter, 90
Tonight I can write the lightest lines., 175
Touch with your finger, 315
Toward the empty earth, 141
Trim my hoofs!, 302
Two curved tortoise-shell combs, 326

U

Under the gold and chalk and brick, beside, 291
Under the high rooms, 132
Up in this quiet room here, reading your letter, 119

W

Walking last night in the drought-country dark, 359
Water, 199
We've been at home four years, in a kind of peace, 49
We all heard the alarm. The planes

were out, 43

We are seated on a wide stage. In the
bright-lit, 22

We cut the new day, 295

We didn't know each other, 315

We dream of saving what, 63

Weeds breaking up through stone:, 122

We her countrypeople are
deep asleep, 268

We met for supper in your flat-
bottomed boat., 64

We stand here like trees in the night, 20

We turn in dream, 405

What could you expect, 118

What do I want here, 12

What is pornography? What
is dream?, 205

When I first heard you on
the phone, 410

"When I found where we had crashed,
in the snow, the two of us, 102

When I lost my courage and
my thought, 398

When I was about twenty I went
by myself, 9

When I woke up, my friend, 415

When I woke up, our time was lost.
No standing, 414

When she told me over the telephone
you died, 341

When we get old, they say,
we'll remember, 48

When we started that day, 210

When you came to town, 46

When you die, 254

While you were alive, 293

White paper masks over

their mouths, 235

Who did I write last night?
Leaning, 176

Who died? My mother's body, 208

Who is my lord?, 23

Who watches, 360

Why did you keep finding me where
I was?, 188

Will I miss you, 348

With the winter and mud and shit
roped into your wool, 305

with this dear one you hold, 6

Women, 5

Y

Years circling the same circle:, 212

Yellow apple, 167

You, I, steadying, 214

You, lying across the wide bed,
vertical, 216

You, poem, 272

You. You running across the field., 77

You are in a blind, 266

You   breathless, 262

you came in a dream yesterday, 412

You drew my head, 297

you leapt sometimes, 392

You never hear me, your
letter said., 167

You or I, 85

Your first child was my father, 51

Your hand on my knee, 283

Your letter made me see myself
grown old, 47

Your mouth "appeared to me", 254

Your number is lifting off my hand, 316

Index of First Lines | **451**

Your red eye—, 316

You said, you know what I mean: one
      winter, you looked and saw, 154

You stood in the doorway in
      the snow:, 215

You take the card of your self out, 174

You waited 4 Ever, 302

You waking to me, 24

You wanted to see Achill Island, 21

You were picking through a
      trash bag, 394

You were willing to like me, and I did
      something, 175

You   who I don't know   I don't
      know how to talk to you, 144

You're gone in the day time, 406

Numbered First Lines

5 a.m., 157

ABOUT THE AUTHOR

Jean Valentine was born in Chicago, earned her B.A. from Radcliffe College, and lived most of her life in New York City. She won the Yale Younger Poets Award for her first book, *Dream Barker*, in 1965. *Door in the Mountain: New and Collected Poems 1965 - 2003* won the 2004 National Book Award for Poetry.

Jean was the State Poet of New York for two years, starting in the spring of 2008. She received the 2009 Wallace Stevens Award from the Academy of American Poets, and also received a Guggenheim Fellowship and awards from the NEA, The Bunting Institute, The Rockefeller Foundation, The New York Council for the Arts, and The New York Foundation for the Arts, as well as the Maurice English Prize, the Teasdale Poetry Prize, and The Poetry Society of America's Shelley Memorial Prize in 2000. In 2014 she was given an award for exceptional accomplishment in literature from the American Academy of Arts and Letters. She was awarded Yale University's Bollingen Prize for Poetry in 2017.

She taught at Sarah Lawrence College, the Graduate Writing Program of New York University, Columbia University, and the 92nd Street Y in Manhattan.

Jean Valentine died on December 29, 2020, in New York, NY. She was 86.

Recent Titles from Alice James Books

Song of My Softening, Omotara James

Theophanies, Sarah Ghazal Ali

Orders of Service, Willie Lee Kinard III

The Dead Peasant's Handbook, Brian Turner

The Goodbye World Poem, Brian Turner

The Wild Delight of Wild Things, Brian Turner

I Am the Most Dangerous Thing, Candace Williams

Burning Like Her Own Planet, Vandana Khanna

Standing in the Forest of Being Alive, Katie Farris

Feast, Ina Cariño

Decade of the Brain: Poems, Janine Joseph

American Treasure, Jill McDonough

We Borrowed Gentleness, J. Estanislao Lopez

Brother Sleep, Aldo Amparán

Sugar Work, Katie Marya

Museum of Objects Burned by the Souls in Purgatory, Jeffrey Thomson

Constellation Route, Matthew Olzmann

How to Not Be Afraid of Everything, Jane Wong

Brocken Spectre, Jacques J. Rancourt

No Ruined Stone, Shara McCallum

The Vault, Andrés Cerpa

White Campion, Donald Revell

Last Days, Tamiko Beyer

If This Is the Age We End Discovery, Rosebud Ben-Oni

Pretty Tripwire, Alessandra Lynch

Inheritance, Taylor Johnson

The Voice of Sheila Chandra, Kazim Ali

Arrow, Sumita Chakraborty

Country, Living, Ira Sadoff

Hot with the Bad Things, Lucia LoTempio

Witch, Philip Matthews

Neck of the Woods, Amy Woolard

Little Envelope of Earth Conditions, Cori A. Winrock

Aviva-No, Shimon Adaf, Translated by Yael Segalovitz

Half/Life: New & Selected Poems, Jeffrey Thomson

Odes to Lithium, Shira Erlichman

Here All Night, Jill McDonough

Alice James Books is committed to publishing books that matter. The press was founded in 1973 in Boston, Massachusetts to give women access to publishing. As a cooperative, authors performed the day-to-day undertakings of the press. The press continues to expand and grow from its formative roots, guided by its founding values of access, excellence, inclusivity, and collaboration in publishing. Its mission is to publish books that matter and preserve a place of belonging for poets who inspire us. AJB seeks to broaden our collective interpretation of what constitutes the American poetic voice and is dedicated to helping its artists achieve purposeful engagement with broad audiences and communities nationwide. The press was named for Alice James, sister to William and Henry, whose extraordinary gift for writing went unrecognized during her lifetime.

Designed by Tiani Kennedy

Printed by Sheridan Saline